Postcolonial Discourse
A Study of Contemporary Literature

In same series

New Commonwealth Writing: A Critical Response
M.L. Pandit

Commonwealth Writing: A Study in Expatriate Experience
R.K. Dhawan and L.S.R.K. Sastry, ed.

Centering the Margins: Perspectives on Literatures in English from India, Africa, Australia
Cynthia vanden Driesen

Critical Studies in Commonwealth Literature
K. Venkata Reddy

Recent Commonwealth Literature (2 vols)
Dhawan, Dhamija, Shrivastava, ed.

Commentaries on Commonwealth Poetry and Drama
S. Ramaswamy

Commentaries on Commonwealth Fiction
S. Ramaswamy

The Novels of V.S. Naipaul: Quest for Order and Identity
N. Ramadevi

The Novels of V.S. Naipaul
Shashi Kamra

Canadian Literature Today
R.K. Dhawan, ed.

Perspectives on Canadian Fiction
Sudhakar Pandey, ed.

Postcolonial Discourse

A Study of Contemporary Literature

Edited by

R.K. Dhawan

PRESTIGE

Published by
Prestige Books
3/28, East Patel Nagar
New Delhi 110 008

ISBN: 81-7551-033-1

1997

Photo Typesetting by
Pivot Computers
Delhi 110 006

Printed at
CHAMAN ENTERPRISES
1603, PATAUDI HOUSE,
DARYA GANJ, NEW
DELHI-110 002

Contents

Colonialism and Literature

HARRICHAND ITWARU

> Histories are more than voices, but voices contain many histories. My speaking here is the speaking of the voices and experiences whose resonation I am.

The introduction of English literature in the education of those whom the English colonizer held in bondage in the labour camps of the British Empire, euphemistically called colonies and plantations, was far from being a benign or a benevolent act. It was not instituted for the presumed good of those on whom this project was implemented. It would be absurd to assume that the dominator-abuser-exploiter had the well-being of those being dominated. Yet this absurdity continues to prevail. Its continuing existence demonstrates the success of the ideological ploy of colonial domination, the project of psychic transformation and disfiguration where the dominated have been persuaded to love their dominator, to identify themselves in relation to their dominator's definition of themselves.

This literature, as I have pointed out in *Closed Entrances*, was insidious and enchanting. It was there in every childhood Reader we were required to read: the Royal Reader, the Macmillan Reader, the Kate and Lay Reader. These selected stories prepared us for the formal study of literature—where to read was to be taken in an imaginary world away from the eloquence of lotus-grown silences to the teachings the civilizing English used to instruct its empire-children in admiration and obedience where purity was said to be as white as the snow we did not know, where important things happened in castles and palaces and royal courts in imperial intrigues and cunning we were to think were true of "the human condition."

This "human condition" did not include us. It was to be found in the literature which spoke of the winter of English Christian-toting people's civilized discontent, their hatred of the unchristian whom they castigated as barbaric and uncivilized, and thus deserving of studied

English disparagement. It told of these civilized white people's pleasures and loves, especially their murderous love of war and killing in their greed for wealth and power. This literature sang eulogies to the English spring, which presumably was also a civilized and Christian occurrence, unlike the uncivilized regions of treacherous monotonous heat, the heart of darkness my world in the sun was deemed to be. It spoke of the midsummernights' frolics of English kings and queens, of handsome charming and brave and wise princes and beautiful lovelorn dutiful princesses dreaming of them. It spoke of noble dukes and duchesses, noble lords and ladies, and the happiness of their obsequious and sycophantic servants.

And we were expected to admire these, to find in their words and actions the wisdom through which the governance of our lives was to be informed. I was supposed to admire the insights of these exemplars of Empire, to draw instructive lessons from the offerings of their literature. It did not matter that my world, my life, my experiences would never, could never correspond to any of these alien English literary obsessions. I was supposed to dream of them nevertheless, to see, to be persuaded to see in them the virtues of truth and beauty and wisdom as the properties and qualities of white people, particularly British white people. My normalcy of life worlds away was an embarrassment of sameness where nothing of significance came from or ever could in this parlance of thought, important only as sharp contrast to the climes in which the self declared finer and elegant and noble were nurtured.

In this literature we were told that in Great Britain some men are born great, some achieve greatness, some have greatness thrust upon them. It did not say what this wonderful quality of greatness was that we should so like it, but to be born great it was clear one necessarily had to be of noble English or European blood. This certainly completely excluded us, and demeaned as inferiors, we were continually being educated to think in our midst there was no one to whom greatness could ever be attributed. Among us no one was "born great." It was madness to think anyone from our lowly realm could ever achieve greatness, much less have "greatness thrust upon them." Besides, what was this greatness that some had it "thrust upon them"? Who was this benevolent bestower of greatness?

Greatness was not to be found among the uncivilized and the underdeveloped. Greatness was over there, in civilized Great Britain and civilized Europe, and we, the uncivilized, the underdeveloped, were required to have a proper respect for civilized and civilizing Great Britain's heroes and their marauding deeds, their acts of piracy they called "adventure," the slaughter and robbery across seas and continents and the peoples of our ancestry. We were to see in the actions and resolutions of these white invaders matters of universal importance, and to write as eloquently as we could of these proclaimed universal truths.

Like England's Shakespeare, "noble" thoughts and "noble" deeds were to be admired, sought after without our recognition that this was in effect also our upholding of that class of privileged Britons who were of titular pre-eminence above all others in Britain—the British nobility—who in conjunction with their status and rank in the order of exploitation were also being imbued, as Shakespeare habitually accords them, with profoundness, wisdom, goodness to the point in which, as in Shakespeare's *Hamlet, Prince of Denmark*, even a face (the Prince's, of course) is deemed noble. And when many of these lords and ladies of the British way went out to maintain the Empire's occupation in its various outposts and colonies, when they lorded their will in pillage and plunder and rape and murder as they thought fit, we were expected to think their victims were culprits who deserved the cruelty inflicted on them, and that those noble and Great Britons were courageous, indeed heroes and champions, worthy of our admiration.

There was no one in our midst to whom this "condition" applied. Did it mean we were not the human "the human condition" was all about? The innocence of this question touched nevertheless upon a vital truth. We were excluded from whatever "the human condition" meant, but we were being indoctrinated from afar, distanced in our unlettered unliterary uncivilized and embarrassing primitivity, to admire what the great and the proud and the good and the superior British and Europeans were doing.

But to derive personal meaning from this was to falsify our sense of ourselves and our realities, to develop an antagonism, even hatred toward ourselves while at the same time admiring the oppressor's world. This is one of the dimensions of psychic transformation as psychic disfiguration.

This literature, understandably, dealt with what was relevant and important to the culture of its making, not ours. When it warbled of fields of daffodils and lily of the valley and sweet eglantine we did not know, it did not have us in mind. It sang of what it knew and thought it knew, the singing of nightingales and larks we never heard, the supremacist ecstasy of "the best school of all" somewhere there in important England, not the zinc-roofed two floor building we had our schooling in. But when this literature is used as required reading upon whose knowledge you passed or failed in your education—then this reading itself becomes the kidnapping of the intellect, a form of psychic splintering in the psychic torture at work here where the disfiguration of the self results in the unreasonableness there is in the violated loving the violator.

This kidnapping, this ensnarement of the intellect is in the mandatory reading, for example, of the adventurous stories of the English in their murderous plunder for gold and other precious items from the peoples and places in our part of the world. It is reading this and admiring the English empire-hero, but more important, it is reading this and not recognizing who the dreadful natives are, not seeing how we are placed in this.

The art and craft of writing, the telling of a persuasive story, the publication, reading and teaching of this, are acts of participation in certain forms of thought which make up the history of the people and place in which the literary imaginary emerges. Despite the problems in the identification of national and regional literatures, these works say a great deal of the thinking which informs the actions of the peoples in these places. More often than not they affirm and thus celebrate these features. Hence their importance in the perpetuation of highly valued ideas and attitudes among such peoples. These literatures are some of the means through which the culture in the making contemplates itself, mythologizes its history, justifies its centralizing preoccupations, constructs a vision of itself through which it gathers momentum and guards against obstacles as it seeks to ensure the conditions favourable to its notion of its own well-being. This is particularly true of nation-states active in the ecstasies of imperialist grandiosities.

We must be careful of that grand euphemism which claims that literature is merely a work of the imagination. What is imagined, the imaginary itself, the emphases in it, the use to which this has been put in terms of my history and others in similar circumstances, the perception of my very existence is what this trap, this trope of thought which requires my admiration of the heroic English men and women, works to undermine. Against these protagonists of civilization I do not exist, I am the anguished absence, a confusion of silence.

This has consequences that go beyond the problem of the divided self, the splitting of the self in two opposing directions. It is part of the momentum of the disfiguring of the self, produced through the making of the culture of psychic disfiguration where schooling obedience to the oppressor takes on notions of personal well-being and the negation of the self is not seen. It must never be forgotten or ignored that colonialism is also the colonization of the mind, the invasion of the psyche in whose conquest the culture of compliant loyalty, convinced of its own inferiority, is reproduced and maintained in the very institutions which make up colonial society.

The schooling that education actually was, taught us to accept the infantile posture of admiring the occupier, to enjoy the occupation without seeing what was happening, without understanding what the project was all about. Our task was to learn to read and write, to help us find a good job. That was what was to be done, and to do it was to have pride in our achievement, to have dignity in knowing we were doing the sensible thing.

This was a particular instrumentalization of learning. Learning as the instrument through which the occupation legitimated its stranglehold. Nothing new, this. Europe's philosophers of war have made a heinous art in their approval of this infamy. The occupied should be taught to love the occupier. In this way the rule of the occupation will be less resisted, hence more effective, more lasting. The colonizing British and their colonizing European counterparts have demonstrated the destructive success of this strategy where they went in their delusions of grandeur to conquer and occupy in the name of their greedy majesties and their blood-thirsty self-proclaimed superior civilization.

This education taught us in admiring our occupiers to love what we did not know and to despise what we did, what we knew intimately, and this included ourselves. We were the inferior, the embarrassing inferior, and it was our lot to both endure and despise this. This was our psychic affliction.

This education taught us to love a place we did not know, but knew enough of to admire, to feel good to be associated with, even proud. To do this was to somehow go beyond our inferiority, to dream of greatness without knowing what greatness was, what this dream of greatness meant to us, or how was it we were dreaming this dream, and whose dream was it we were dreaming.

We were dreaming the dream of oppression. A dream which dreams itself in unctuous and heady scenarios of success concealing the cruel deception at work. A dreaming desire dreaming of becoming like the occupier, whose world we were to accept was in and of itself great, where this quality of greatness was without question to be found.

Every book this education taught us came from this particular occupier's world, variously and grandiosely called England, Britain, Great Britain, the United Kingdom and with an embarrassing imaginary fondness and intimacy the UK, the Motherland, the Centre, the Seat of the Empire whose obedient children one and all we were, who must always heed Her call.

Sadistic empire ecstasy. Harmonious infantilism.

This education told us the men and women of Britain were brave, heroic, civilized, great. We inferiors were to admire the brave and daring exploits of the sailors and officials of that great state, Great Britain. It told us the difficulties the great men and women of this Great Britain had dealing with the peoples of my ancestry were because we were treacherous, barbaric, unchristian, unclean, disrespectful of law and order, illiterate, incapable of governing ourselves, uncivilized, and therefore were in need of the strong arm of authority from Great Britain's monarchs and officials and their loyal killers their great generals and admirals, their great army and navy victorious on land and sea and in the air, their lords and ladies, their great thinkers whose ideas of superiority furnished the barbarism of the British violation of peoples and cultures wherever it went to occupy.

Of course, it was never said in this manner. This barbarism flattered itself in the narcissism of gentility. Its crudity required politeness. These bearers of greatness and decency felt they deserved respect, and especially from us. We were supposed to be respectful of them. And sadly many of us were.

This education taught me to sing in respectful strains, God Save Our Gracious King, and later, God Save Our Gracious Queen when Elizabeth II of England was coronated. Three cheers for the Red White and Blue! and other Empire Ecstasy songs. Three cheers to Her Gracious Majesty. I was to hold my cup with the imprint of the face of this Queen of the British Empire on it and to feel she had personally sent it for me, to hold this cup and sing, Rule Britannia Rule, Britannia rule the waves, Britons will never be slaves. And we all did.

Like the others I did not know what a Briton was. Could it be that as children of the Empire we too were among those Britons since we were not slaves and, as far as we were concerned, never would be? It did not occur to us that the Britons so celebrated were actually at one time proud enslavers and upholders of human bondage across oceans and continents. We were taught that the British abolished slavery, and for this we should wish for the continuing reign of British prosperity, and whenever we uttered this occupier's refrain, "Long Live Great Britain, Long live Her Royal Majesty," we were to feel proud and honourable.

For many of us there was no pleasure in this kind of singing which we were forced to learn at school. We were physically assaulted by our teachers to sing praises to the continuation of the British occupation. These teachers' ready whips and canes repeated, with our parents' problematic approval, that form of torture inflicted on resistant enslaved human beings long before our time. It was also the manifestation of the cruelty in that infamous English pedagogic adage of tyranny: spare the rod and spoil the child. Flogging children to do what they did not understand, what they were not persuaded of. Forcing compliance through physical abuse. Torture in the euphemism corporal punishment. In the name of education. A nice school-teaching job.

Empire ecstasy. Brutal satisfaction in the infliction of pain on the weak and defenceless to facilitate the brutal order intrinsic to the occupation. Committed by the agents of the project of schooling obedience, school teachers, supposedly decent people, beating children with whips and belts to sing praises to the occupier. A singing alien to the Hindi bhajans, mantras and popular Indian songs we adored and sang, always out of school, away from the world of that schooling which strictly disapproved of such uncivilized and uncivilizing utterances.

These are examples of the production of the culture of self negation, necessary for the greater continuation of colonialism.

That special cup I had to hold up and sing to, that coronation cup, was a magical item, a very talisman of beauty. My mother kept it for years with her select three pieces of glassware we never used. The cup with the face of the Queen had this special place in our home and all those homes fortunate enough to have it. Our colonization was our pathetic source of pride.

This education was education, I was told. It was special, even sacred. It was not politics. It was above politics. It was objective. It was education. It was not to be questioned, it was to be learned. And there was so much to learn. Only fools and troublemakers questioned education, resisted learning. Only the nogoods did not want to improve their intelligence, those with no future, no ambition, those who had no interest in being someone, those who would work and die in the sugarcane fields, children of misery labouring in misery until they could labour no more. It was about teaching and learning. The principles and practices of this education written by select British educators mattered. And it was my responsibility to adapt to these. That was what was going to save us, that was what was going to save me, if I wanted to matter.

The required readings of English literature took us away from the play of life in us and amidst us in the struggle for survival which our living had been made into by the imperial occupier. It ignored the voices in us. It taught us to disregard the lament of the speaking dead, the sweat the blood the body of memory in the ground and footpaths of our daily existences. It took us away from the ripening of rice in us, it took us outside of ourselves, away from ourselves, away from our mothers' and fathers' gaze, it deafened us against their speaking. It turned our thinking towards a deceptive inwardness, a thinking which looked towards England for meaning.

This is a delusional gaze. It is the opposite of colonialism's imperial delusions of grandeur. This delusional gaze is the gaze of dependence. It compliments the imperial gaze, the colonizing gaze, validates it, and thus furthers the designation of the inferiority of the successfully colonized. This amounts to the literary induction of domination.

The delusional gaze (among other grievous concerns) approves of the atrocity of conquest, does not see who is it who is conquered, and is not concerned with the implications of conquest. There is a tradition in the reading of English and European literatures which refuses to consider the importance of the imperializing vision in many of these works. This refusal is in itself an example of the presence of a studied attitude of presumed aloofness from the "political"—as if writers and the things and people they write about are outside of the history of thought in which they have grown. This attitude, this disciplinary silence which stops critical inquiry into an imperialist nation-state's practices and the literature which is produced within it which affirms its principal political action, needs scrutiny. The claim that "literature is above this," is no longer tenable. For this is one of the ways the culture of imperialism is kept intact.

Literature (and by this I am referring to English literature and literature written in English) is not exempt from such institutionalizing assumptions and political function, despite claims to the contrary. The approach to literature is rife with mythologies governing its production and reception. There is an order which is enshrined in much of what constitutes literary knowledge. And in the colonializing project it meant learning to imitate, to memorize and quote from your English authority. This literature, regardless of whatever might have occasioned its writing, when used in the context of the imperialist project to which it has been put, became the teaching of a particular sensibility, an attitude of obeisance to and admiration of the literary aesthetic of the culture of the occupying force, a literary politicization of domination, one of the actions of the "triumphal art of Empire."[1]

The triumphal in this art works in the enchantment of the imagination, the titillation and entrapment of the intellect to derive meaning within the imaginary articulated in the scenarios of each select text, and subsequently the world inscribed in them *as well as the world inscribing them*. It is assumed in this premise that our thinking must necessarily be realized within the occupier's frames of references, that these perspectives should govern the ways we reflect on our condition. And in so doing to not pay heed to the fundamental differences in the circumstances in which we are deemed subordinate, our realities subservient to the principals as well as the principles of the super-ordinating imperial order.

This literature was not taught with a view to the development of the critical imagination of those of us who were coerced into reading it. It would be too much to expect this of the occupation, of any occupation. Rather this literature was used to intensify the authority of the occupier's culture, and as such its exaltation was also the arrogant manifestation of English authoritarian practice in the guise of literary advocacy, literary knowledge. Literary criticism as it was propounded provided the conceptual tools through which certain English academic literary authorities established the methods and procedures governing the modes of reading, and the analysis of these.

They were telling us how we should read these chosen works of theirs, how we should think when we imbued ourselves in such presumed higher thought. Our perspectives based on our experience, our vision, was always outside of the allowable, not even tolerated. To dare to say anything seriously critical of these works being lorded on us as great literature was to suffer the punishment and ignominy of failure. We mattered only in relation to our being able to demonstrate how well we could imitate these English authorities. To have success was to show how clever we were in remaining within the limits of such benevolent scholarly allowance, how well we could practice an *imitative intellectuality* in which there prevailed the odious paternalism pertaining to the English notion of the proper ways of doing this.

This paternalism required the infantilization of the conquered subject-mass to which I have earlier referred—the children of the empire, who one and all must also be obedient, always ready and eager to please by identifying memorizing and quoting their English authority as demonstration of their learning, by reciting texts from English poems, plays and novels and ensuring the appropriate inflections and intonations, and by being accordingly ashamed of the speech and the peoples in whose speaking they live.

Be literate: imitate.

This was not how it was said, but this was what was happening. To think of what was considered higher things was to imitate as much as possible the thinking of our designated betters, and these writers we were dubiously fortunate enough to read were, in the order of the occupation's ranking, our betters. In this way imitation served to perpetuate subordination, with the more absorbing the imitation the greater the importance of the source being imitated.

This is a form of enchantment.

Enchantment does not allow for self-reflection. The enchanted is under the power of the enchanter. The relationship is a hypnogogic one for the enchanted. And enchantment with the occupier's world, however half-dreamed, however imagined, is where the seduction in imitation holds its fatal ploy. The mask of this enchantment is imprinted with notions of dignity and pride, but we should be careful of these. What do they mean? What is it that is happening?

The disturbing truth is that the more you keep doing it, the more imitative you are, the more dependent you are. In the face of the person or source being imitated the imitator is always of lesser importance, always subservient, always unoriginal. Here imitation constructs the self as false, as inauthentic, as always inferior to that which is being imitated. Imitation is the embellishment of power relations in which the illusion of authenticity drives the imitator to enjoy being controlled. This is necromancy: the hypnogogic cortege ecstatically bearing the death of the independent self. The oblivion march.

Imitation reinforces dependency, encourages an infantile posturing where the select children of the empire, the educated, are now to flatter themselves of their presumed superior knowledge and self-importance even as they absorb themselves in and are absorbed by an *imitative intellectuality*.

Consider, among others, the following:

— the writing of experience outside of the cultural codifications of Britain or Europe to fit within the structures of English/European genres of expression.
— the declaration of William Shakespeare as a universal genius. Collapse of historical and cultural differences or cultural imperialism?
— the application of the term "novel" to refer to works of literature which are outside of the allowances of the genre of the novel. The resistance to acknowledging articulations outside of the prescribed format for the writing which emerges outside of the sensibility of the novel-form fabrication of meaning.
— the insistence on plot and character as literary modes of perception. What happens to a work when it is dissected into character and plot? What is "character'? Whose character? What's a flawed character? What assumptions are there in the construction of the notion of "character"?
— the habitual comparison of writers outside of Britain and Europe with British or European writers. The troubling assumption that there is always a British or a European as the authority, against whom or like whom works of difference are measured.

— the retainance of colonization as the mode of perception in the terms "Commonwealth literature," and the more recent, "Postcolonial literature."

Reflection into these would reveal the workings of a colonialism still active.

NOTE

1. Homi K. Bhabha, "The Other Question: Difference, Discrimination and the Discourse of Colonialism," in *Out There: Marginalization and Contemporary Cultures*, Russel Furguson et al (Cambridge, Massachussets: The Mit Press, 1992), p. 72.

Postcolonial Discourse: Doing away with Labels

AMINA KISHORE

The history of English studies and the Indian literary criticism in English reveals the continued hangups of both teachers and scholars and critics about English language, English cultural and political hegemony and its insidious domination over the Indian psyche as well as literary performance. At the same time, there was at no point in history any slackening of interest in creative writing in English or critical readings into English—including the literature produced abroad and on the home soil.

Labels are enterprising critics' hobby-horses. Postcolonialism, Neo-colonialism, feminist critiques, now lately patriarchal discourse etc. have been coined and justified in powerful arguments. The language of criticism has acquired a sophistication which is admirable. But the competitiveness in this field is showing an alarming tendency of each label getting an overnight replacement by a newer and more fascinating alternative.

The trend of historicity in literary criticism in combination with a quickening inquisitiveness into the nature of language use as a sound yardstick of evaluation—has concentrated the attention of the critics of the last decade upon explorations into discourse strategies, especially in fiction.

The common critical enterprise is to embark upon a hunt for that strategy and literary device in fictional works which supports the respective hypotheses of the different schools of thought. For example postmodernists like to identify as devices the following:

> Self-reflexivity, Intertextuality, Allegory, Pastiche, Historicism, and Diverse Narrative (Narrative complexity, merging of high and low literatures), e.g., in the critique of Ondaatje's 'The English Patient' (*Literature Alive*, V, 3), Nilufer Bharucha refers to the mixing of narrative tones—the high and the low.

The group of critics who see all fiction from newly free nations as postcolonial discourse find what they consider to be unique literary strategies in select fictional works. One of the strategies identified by them is what is termed as Historicising postcolonial writers' attempt to repossess their colonial history and to rewrite it through overt evocations of postcolonial discourse.

When Mark Twain mixes the educated American stand of the white boy Tom with the primeval longings of the river-bound free spirit of the urchin Huck Finn, it is merely seen as a celebration of the time spirit of America.

When the novelist William Faulkner employs the device of 'connecting' the disparate American features of the white master and the Negro slave—he takes quite great pains to suggest a marked degree of respect for the natural strengths of the Negro race which not only endures but contains within itself the will to sustain the white race. And, the critics of Faulkner's fiction are quite satisfied, generally, with the humanistic evaluation without ascribing any conflict-indicating motifs to Faulkner's narratives.

The critics of American fiction (which is also an output of an erstwhile colonized race) do not feel the urgent and continued need to speak of the story of restlessness, loneliness and defiance of Huck Finn as a colonial or postcolonial traumatic discourse; perhaps because the high success story of the Americans overpowers its not so very ancient colonial memory thoroughly!!!

Postcolonial discourse is a hot-house plant which is being nurtured until the fad dies out. The critics are straining their 'Eye Spies' antennae to the extreme limit and decoding fictional narratives of postcolonial times in such a way as to decipher strategies of postcolonial discourse. These members of the postcolonial school believe that all authors are embarked on a suicidal linear movement which imposes the possibility of a single line of historic as well as literary tradition. To put it simply, the postcolonialist voices give out that all narratives are overt or covert diatribes against the humiliation of race in terms of political, religious, social and above all, literary dependency. These assessments, in their defensive zeal, tend to find subjugation of the colonist on all counts. In the creative voices of the new writers of fiction in English, in the imagery used, in the narrative strategies, everywhere and in every literary gesture are alarmist signs of colonial repressions as the critics would let us see it.

From this point of view, the critic will have to pinpoint certain literary strategies which are the exclusive innovation or invention of writers of a certain period. The critic then will have to follow a sweeping mode and declare all literature of the period as broadly 'connected to' and influenced by the historic actuality. Individual differences, myth, universality of literature, the ahistoric and timeless quality of creativity—all these possibilities get ruled out, once total historicity becomes the yardstick of standardization.

The second definition of postcolonialism is based on the conceptual aspect of the term. As critical terminology the term colonialism acquires ahistoric features. Colonialist discourse is associated with the politics of interrelationships as and when they are affected by patterns of authority-subjugation. Looked at from this point of view, it is easy to find strains of postcolonial discourse in any text which thematically or otherwise employs the interplay of class, gender or hierarchical relationships.

A third approach, and to a large extent, a rider to the historic conceptualization of the term 'postcolonial' suggests to the prefix 'post' the meaning of a conditioner for the term 'colonial' so that a sense of opposition between two ideologies is created.

Taken in this sense, the suffix can be taken to represent a relationship with colonialism either of succession or supercession. Critics like Helen Tiffin and Viney Kirpal are critical of the western inclination to read Indian literature in English only from the colonialist point of view. Helen Tiffin's criticism of Malcolm Bradbury is quite clear on this count in her essay 'Commonwealth Literature and Comparative Methodology.' So also is her recognition of the impulse of decolonization present as 'prime impulse' in all postcolonial literatures. (Ref: 'Post-colonialism, Post-Modernism and the Rehabilitation of Post-Colonial History' in the *Journal of Commonwealth Literature.*)

The main feature of the postcolonialist school of criticism is that it assumes a successionist or processionist stances on part of the writers of the Commonwealth nations. The irony here is that it has succeeded in heading a procession of critics from the Commonwealth countries. The absence of known critical tools or clarity about the nature of the critical tools which can be suitably applied and the search for a viable and credible critical idiom, has sent the western critics on a journey of slogan hunting. And the local critic has not lagged behind in picking up exotic voices from the west. It should be pointed out that 'postcolonialism' as a critical ideology is usually expressed in terms of disquiet. The critics of this school are heard lamenting the loss of cultural identity or 'cultural memory' as Devy puts it. Their main purpose seems to be to rebuild upon the pre-colonial past glories; and to point out the need to break free from contemporary 'colonization of the mind.' But such a noble zeal goes awry because of the single-minded thesis that *all* literature of the postcolonial times essentially suffers from the malady of a repressed and fractured colonized psyche.

To ascribe colonial attitudes (the term 'colonialism' is obliquely capable of standing for both the colonizer and the colonized!!) to the writers of the colonized nations is to neglect the pre-colonial creative setting and to assume a total amnesia on part of these writers. The colonial experience is exploited artistically by many a writer of these erstwhile colonies. In these cases, the experience becomes an additional source of material which feeds the genre of fiction and accords it the realistic tenor that it aspires for and deserves.

It is equally easy to demonstrate that almost all the narrative strategies which the postcolonialist critics like to enumerate under the head of 'postcolonial discourse,' are devices which one encounters even in the novels of the pre-colonial times. Viney Kirpal, in her essay 'What is Modern Third World Novel?' in one of the issues of *Journal of Commonwealth Literature,* mentions the following generalizations about the Third World novel which distinguish it from the western novel: (a) 'Loose episodic structure' which is said to be the 'Fable and Folk Tale Form.' Examples of Mulk Raj Anand, Achebe, Naipaul, Soyinka and even Tutuola are cited as users of this strategy. The implication is that such device would have to be taken as the Commonwealth writer's wish to break free from the western hegemony by setting up his own fund of native strategies.

However the logical literary memory is certain to yield a large number of western examples which also possess the strategy of 'loose episodic structure' and follow some form of native traditional narrative. For example, the structure of *Sound and Fury* is episodic and exploits the biblical genre.

(b) Proverbialisms, metaphors, song and dance which seem to distinguish the novels of the colonies are features which lend these novels a ritualistic, timeless and mythical quality. But, these features are not unique to the novels from the lately independent nations. Mark Twain's novels exploit, as do many other novels of the Frontier, the rhythms of the native speech and its idiomatic richness. The interweaving of song and dance into the narrative is again a feature which has been noticed to be a device in many a western novel like Hardy's *Mayor of Casterbridge.*

My whole contention is that, to read fictional works as discourse is a broad critical activity. The conditioning of the term by ideological or politically oriented labelling limits the scope of interpretation of a text. The fictive text is a reality which emerges after the culling together of many actualities of the human experiential spectrum. This very complexity of its make-up allows it to be interpreted in innumerable ways while retaining the cohesion and unity of text. It will be wise to remember that no fictional work should be subjected to the concept of total alignment or total dependency on some hypothetical 'master text.' If there are echoes of other texts in some novels of the new nations (especially of the postcolonial time), such a presence should be honoured as a manifestation of that timeless narrative device—intertextuality. Doing otherwise would be to push the issue beyond logic and demonstrates the politics of interpretation.

Selective and tailored hermeneutics can yield any result which is desired by the interpreter. Here I would like to refer to the latest, increasingly popular and sensational critical exercise of finding an archetypal father figure, Prospero, to stand in for the image of the arch colonizer; and Caliban as the myth generating literary persona of the arch colonized. This whole exercise is extremely satisfying for the new faddist of postcolonial discourse since it obtains for him an immediate corroboration of his thesis with regard to the politics of colonization and its effect on speech (taken in a metonymic sense). Caliban's idiomatic and idiosyncratic rebelliousness is marked out by these interpretations as an example of postcolonial consciousness. Such an exercise indicates the ahistoric nature of such rebellions and places them in a right perspective of the primeval longings of the human spirit for freedom and its refusal to be contained.

My contention is again that the investigation into postcolonial discourse is one of the possibilities of interpretation and can be applied to authors of all ages, nationalities and gender. *Prometheus Unbound* will yield as much material of recapture of self against a relegation, as does the figure of Satan in Milton. Across the continent, the central motif of O'Neill's *Hairy Ape* can also be read as a postcolonial expression of extreme protest. The theorist is always in search of a terminology which can find closest proximity to his latest and more attentive readings into conceptual problems of narration and creativity. He endeavours to make his argument lively and credible by the use of textual evidence. Unfortunately, the significance and independence of the text gets subsumed under the logic of the moment offered by the latest interpretative idiom and its slick sophistication. The history of criticism has been one of multiple schools of opinion and counter-opinion. A bedlam of disparatenesses has surfaced but happily, the creative act has gone on; and, fed less by theory or ideology and more by that undefinable urge of creativity, it lives a full life.

Self-conscious, pragmatic and ideologous novelists are few and far between. Most fictionists prefer to maintain silence on theoretical issues and prefer to desist from commenting on their own texts. This natural reticence combines well with the strategic use of silences and absences within the text itself, and is the sensitive writer's private homage to the independence of the created work and also to the reader's liberty to read his own meanings into discourse.

I would agree with G.N. Devy's criticism of the colonial epistemology. He squarely places the responsibility on the Indian critic who operates under the pressure of a felt need to protest against what he senses to be allegations of colonial hang over, and yet follows exotic banners just so that he can join an authenticated group. Western critical hegemony does play a covert but subtle and subversive role in guiding the trend of evaluation of Indian literature in English. Local critics who have been conscious of this subtle arm-twisting, have reacted rather violently by formulating frantic defences in favour of what they prefer to call 'nationalism' in the new literatures. The terms used by this defence group, Search for Identity, Discovery of the Past etc., carry a thinly veiled desperation and lack of self-confidence. Half baked and fortuitous 'critical' statements like "Matthew Arnold in a Sari," said to have been authored by someone of no subsequent significance, named Gordon Bottomley, have the surprising power of sending the Indian critic and writer into a flurry of offended self-esteem. Unless and until criticism breaks free from the colonizing habit of mind, and unless it rises above the concerns of 'self' and 'the other,' these misreadings of the text of life will continue.

Literature of the Raj: Colonial Discourse and Postcolonial Readers

NILUFER E. BHARUCHA

The British connection with India began with tenuous embassies at the court of the Mughals in the seventeenth century, strengthened into trading ties in the eighteenth century and then developed into a full-blown Empire by the middle of the nineteenth century. When India wrenched itself away from the imperial embrace in 1947, the two nations had been in contact on Indian soil for nearly three hundred and fifty years. In the wider perspective of Indian history, which stretches back thousands of years, these three and a half centuries might not have much significance, but in the context of the shaping of modern India's socio-political consciousness, these were crucial years.

This period of India's colonial history tends to be dismissed by its postcolonial heirs. However, it is a period which needs to be re-possessed and understood rather than shunned. The colonial period spawned a vast body of writing and it is this colonial discourse which has to be deconstructed to arrive at a better understanding of the past and through it the present. As Ashcroft, Gareth and Tiffin[1] have said, colonial texts need to be dismantled to expose the signifying systems and reveal the mechanisms for silencing and marginalizing the colonial subject.

The Anglo-Indians (the term favoured by the British in India as a self-definition, until it was appropriated by the Eurasians), wrote copiously—letters, memoirs, diaries, novels, poems and histories. These writings have been neglected by Indians. Few Indian scholars have worked at deciphering the ideological value of these texts.[2] Most research in this area has been undertaken by Western scholars who lack the special privilege afforded to Indians—the "Insider-Outsider" view of imperial discourse.[3]

Not just Indian scholars but postcolonial Indian society at large needs to engage with the imperial experience, for the effect of European imperial domination continues to be felt even in decolonized societies.

It is just that political imperialism has been replaced by cultural and economic imperialism.[4] As a result, vast sections of postcolonial India continue to 'image' themselves in the mirror of Eurocentricism. This image asserted itself most strongly in the Anglo-Indian writing of the nineteenth century. It is in the literature of Anglo-India that we have the full flowering of the concept of what has been termed by Said as Orientalism[5]—the stereotypical definition of the East by the West.

Orientalism is the way in which the West has looked at the East and more importantly tried to make the reality of the East conform to the image of the Orient held by the West. There are at least two definite aspects of Orientalism. One is concerned with the notion of the exotic East: the land of temples, swaying palms, elephants, tigers, jungles, broad rivers and magnificent sunsets. This view stereotypes the Eastern landscape and seeks to control it. The other aspect concentrates on human beings. The Oriental man is reductively portrayed as impulsive, weak, sly, lazy, irrational and childlike. He needs the analytical leadership provided by the Occident to get out of even his own messes. In the past it was colonial rule, today it is the IMF and the World Bank. The Oriental woman is sensual, beautiful, a magnificent symbol of the Occident's fascination with the Orient, a fascination which has definite overtones of the sexual.

It is in this context that the easy availability of Anglo-Indian texts in postcolonial India becomes important. As Naik has bemoaned, Anglo-Indian writing is a fast disappearing commodity and is now available only in a few old university libraries in India. Even these scarce resources are now in danger of succumbing to the ravages of time and silver fish. However, recent Indian reprints by Rupa and Indus (an imprint of Harper Collins Publishers) have put some of the writing of the Raj, at easily affordable prices, in the hands of a generation of Indians who can approach it without the burden of inferiority imposed on colonized subjects or the ideological baggage of the Nationalists who rejected all things colonial.

The reprints range from fiction, to specific literature on what the Raj perceived as the Mutiny of 1857, to general histories of British India, to Raj Nostalgia literature. Fiction was the favourite form of self-definition for most Anglo-Indians. This is not surprising given the paramount position occupied by the novel in nineteenth century European literature. The Anglo-Indians wrote a large number of novels and short stories. However, until very recently the work of Rudyard Kipling overshadowed that of all other novelists of British India. In fact after Kipling the only other recognized Anglo-Indian novelists are E.M. Forster and Paul Scott. E.M. Forster was not really an Anglo-Indian and wrote only one novel on India—*A Passage to India.* Paul Scott's writing belongs to the Raj Nostalgia genre, rather than to literature of the Raj proper, so in effect Kipling ruled supreme.

This canonical view of Anglo-Indian literature is challenged by the re-discovery of scores of other writers who wrote about their lives in India, their reaction to the country and its inhabitants. The majority of these writers were female—the women of the Raj. They have been given a voice in the collections edited by Saros Cowasjee, *Women Writers of the Raj*[6] and are also well represented in his two other volumes, *Stories from the Raj*[7] and *More Stories from the Raj and After.*[8]

The women of the Raj—the Memsahibs—have been unfairly blamed for one of the major failings of the Raj, i.e. lack of interaction between the races. Critics and creative writers alike, colonial and postcolonial, have painted the Memsahib in the blackest of black.[9] She has been dubbed racist, mean-minded, arrogant and even stupid. Yet it is in the stories and novels of Flora Annie Steel, Alice Perrin, Maud Diver, Bithia Mary Croker, F.E.F. Penny and Ethel W. Savi that we come closest to the reality of the Raj. The Raj was not always, and not for all, the bracing, ego-inflating, libido-magnifying experience that most of Kipling's writings makes it out to be. For the women, the Raj more often meant tears, tragic separation from children or husband (when the children were sent 'home' for education), long empty days and above all sudden deaths. These women were in the double-blind of Victorian patriarchy and rampant colonialism—at one and the same time subordinate and superior.

The dilemma of these women is well captured by Sara Jeanette Duncan in 'A Mother in India.' (Cowasjee, 1982) Also in spite of the male dictum of paternalism towards the natives and contempt for the Eurasians (persons of mixed Indian and British blood), a most genuine desire to connect with both is reflected in the Memsahib's books. In *Lal* and *Heera Nund*, Flora Annie Steel (Cowasjee, 1992) portrays the natives with deep empathy and considerable understanding of the Indian psyche. Flora Annie Steel is in fact a much underrated novelist, who has been denied her rightful place among the 'greats' of Anglo-Indian fiction. Bithia Mary Croker's *The Proud Girl* (Cowasjee, 1992) narrates the tragic tale of a Eurasian girl caught between two worlds—Indian and British.

Yet in spite of these positive aspects, a deconstruction of the Novels of Empire reveals most of the stereotypes of Orientalism, overt or covert; racism and moral self-righteousness. The Indian characters in these novels are usually stereotypes—fakirs, Rajas and the faithful, upright soldiers. There are also the sneaky, unreliable Indians, the 'banias,' the 'babus,' and in the twilight of the Raj, the Nationalists. These Indian characters serve to reinforce the more 'positive' side of the British character, i.e. honesty, integrity and a sense of duty.[10] This naturally bolstered the self-image of the Anglo-Indians and helped them to preserve their sense of identity in a huge overpowering country, which annihilated even as it was sought to be subdued.

However, this colonial discourse, this assertion of superiority of race, culture and civilization, has to be understood for what it is—a self-justifying, a self-defensive and morale-boosting exercise. It is not to be allowed to dictate terms of cultural hegemony in a decolonized social order and set itself up as a touchstone of values, culture and even good taste.

Literature on the Mutiny of 1857 remains an area of colonial discourse where the lines are more clearly drawn and loyalties more clearly defined than in general fiction or other writings. This is even more evident in non-fiction on the Mutiny, than in the fictional representations of those events. Flora Annie Steel's *On the Face of the Waters,*[11] which is a 'Mutiny Novel' is more ambivalent in tone than the *Indus* reprints of Sir George Otto Trevelyan's *Cawnpore*[12] and P.J.O. Taylor's *A Star Shall Fall*[13] and *Chronicles of the Mutiny.*[14] Trevelyan's *Cawnpore* purports to be a factual documentation of the events that have been variously described as 'The Munity' and 'The First War of Independence,' depending on which side of the fence you viewed it from—the British or the Indian. The book focusses on the massacre that took place at Kanpur, the butchering of the beleagured British soldiers, their commanders and their wives and children. They were slaughtered by the sepoys loyal to the Nana Sahib, one of the leaders of the Mutiny. Nana Sahib's culpability, however, has not been proved beyond doubt; especially with regard to the killing of the women and children in the 'Bibigarh.' This was one event in 1857, which most traumatised the British psyche. As Philip Mason has written in a foreword to *Cawnpore*: 'the events of that June in 1857 [in Kanpur], had an effect on English minds similar to that which Jallianwalla Bagh had on Indian minds more than sixty years later.

Trevelyan wrote this book in 1865 when he was only 25 years old. There is therefore much in this text which might have been different had there been a greater time lapse between the actual events and their narration, as well as more maturity in the narrator. For instance there is much gorss simplification in Cawnpore about the reasons for the Mutiny. Trevelyan attributes it largely to the greed and caste arrogance of the Sepoys. He makes little allowance for the role played by the Company's parsimonious attitude, which deprived the sepoy of his foreign allowance—the *butta*—on the conquest of Oudh. So the Sepoys felt aggrieved that their contribution to the conquest of Oudh, instead of being rewarded, led to a pay-cut.

Also, the Sepoy Mutiny of 1857, though not really a War of Independence, was much more than an outcry of peeved soldiers. There was widespread dissatisfaction and insecurity among the landowning classes who felt threatened by the Benthamite zeal of Lord Dalhousie. Yet it would be dangerous to allow Michael Edwardes[15] to dismiss it as 'the reaction of a conservative, tradition-loving section of Indian society to the modernizing zeal of their British conquerors.'

This is colonial discourse at its worst. It arrogates to itself all positive values, while relegating the most negative to 'the other.' The Mutiny was in many ways the outcome of the colonizer's arrogant refusal to accept Indian socio-political customs and values. The Indian tradition of adoption by a King, in the event of his remaining childless, was unacceptable to the British. The ruthless annexation of Indian state after state on the grounds of what the colonial masters considered a lack of legitimate heirs, as in the case of Jhansi, or gross mismanagement and decadent behaviour of the ruler (as perceived by the British) as in Oudh, outraged Indian sensibilities. Moreover, Dalhousie's actions smacked of the 'double-think' of colonial discourse. The alleged depravity of the King of Oudh was ostensibly contrasted with the moral virtues of the conquering race, thereby setting up the value-system of the West in a superior position to that of the East. What was glossed over was the fact that Dalhousie's actions were hardly altruistic. The annexation policy gained for the British large tracts of land and huge revenues.

Trevelyan's stated purpose in writing *Cawnpore* was to do 'some small thing towards the reconciliation of races estranged by a terrible memory.' This 'terrible' aspect of *Cawnpore* has to be squarely faced by the decolonized consciousness. It would be intellectually dishonest to condemn the atrocities of the Jallianwalla Bagh without an eyeball-to-eyeball confrontation with the massacre at Kanpur—both are equally reprehensible. An important element of postcolonial perspectives on colonial texts is the ability to grapple with revisionist Nationalist histories of events in the colonial past. From this angle *Cawnpore* is a touchstone for the postcolonial critic. It has to be dismantled but its essential truth has to be recognized. It is a flawed text but the author has not assigned blame to the Indian side alone. He has very bravely given the context within which he wrote, revealed the role of Europeans who fought with the rebels in Kanpur, as also in Delhi and Lucknow. He has also not flinched from documenting the revenge wreaked on the rebel sepoys by the British—in most cases they were blown to bits from canons.

P.J.O. Taylor's *A Star Shall Fall* and *Chronicles of the Mutiny* enjoy the advantage of temporal distancing and were published as recently as 1991 and 1992. So they are in a sense subject to the ambivalent feelings of guilt and shame about the Raj on the one hand, and on the other, a pride in what the Raj had stood for, i.e., the values of Western civilization and its 'gifts' to the East. This makes these books rather complex and ambiguous texts. Also, what is intriguing about the *Chronicles* is that it is made up of a series of articles which appeared in *The Statesman*, New Delhi, from 1989-1991. *A Star Shall Fall* is a more cohesive re-hash of the above. So the target reader for whom these texts were written was the decolonized Indian. This has obviously imposed a strain on Taylor, who belongs to Philip Mason's generation, a generation born and brought up in imperial England, and with a history of service in India.

The pride and pleasure that Mason took in British India, has in the case of Taylor, to be suppressed. However, it often spurts to the surface of the text in a subversion of his carefully crafted neutrality and 'political correctness.' Nowhere is this more evident than in his portraits of the Nana Sahib and his counsellor Azimullah Khan. The Nana is the stereotypical pleasure-loving oriental despot. Azimullah is the equally typical shifty, untrustworthy Indian who has acquired a veneer of English education and manners, which makes him even more suspect in British eyes.

In addition to this covert racism, Taylor's texts abound in blatantly sexist attitudes towards women, both British and Indian, who featured prominently during the events of 1857. A case in point is the portrait of Miss Wheeler, General Wheeler's daughter by his Indian wife, who went missing during the seige of Kanpur, and was turned into a heroine by the British. Even more tasteless and sexist are the references to Miss Dolly, a European widow, but 'country-born' (a term of abuse in Anglo-India), who kept a brothel and not only entertained rebel sepoys but also spurred them on against the British. The Begum of Oudh is yet another target.

Taylor's populist 'history' is in contrast with the scholarly tone of Michael Edwardes' and Philip Mason's books. Edwardes' *British India 1772-1947* was first published in 1967, barely a generation after the process of decolonization had begun in 1947. Edwardes himself is aware of this shortcoming and makes a reference to it. However, the 1992 reprint of this book has a blurb which continues to plug it as a 'well-documented study' which shows how 'traditional culture imbibed new concepts of law, justice, nationalism, social reforms and English language with enthusiasm.' This is absolutely unacceptable and unforgivable. Even if one is not rabidly 'Nativist,' it is difficult to even begin to comprehend how concepts like law and justice were 'new' to a civilization as old as India, where myth and history celebrate the law and justice of Raja Harishchandra and the Mughals, Akbar and Jehangir. This is even without any reference to the subtle, sophisticated and highly evolved ideological writings of Kautilya, which predate English notions of nation and politics by at least a millennium.

Edwardes' book is unabashedly self-righteous and strident about what it considers the virtues of the British Raj. However, this is not to detract from its value of offering a single volume survey of British India.

More interesting and more important are the books written by Philip Mason. Mason's attitude towards India can be summed up by his dedication of *The Men Who Ruled India* 'to the peoples of India and Pakistan whose tranquillity was our care, whose division our failure, and whose continuance in the family of nations to which we belong is our Memorial.' Here we have the notion of Empire as a sacred trust, the paternalistic overtones of High Imperialism, best show-cased in Kipling's writings, combined with the guilt of having failed this trust, also manifested in serious Raj Nostalgia writings, e.g. Paul Scott's *The Raj Quartet.*[16] Finally there is the continuing feeling of self-congratulation, a justification of the Raj as a civilizing force, which has now metamorphosed itself into the Commonwealth, this is the most insidious aspect of the dedication.

Mason is a prolific writer. As Philip Woodruff he has written novels *(Call the Next Witness, The Wild Sweet Witch),* short stories, children's fiction, historical novels and history. As Philip Mason, after retirement from the Indian Civil Service, he has written on race and race relations, history, biography, a historical novel and also a book on religion.

However, Mason's *magnum opus* remains *The Men Who Ruled India,* brought out in one volume in 1985 and first published in 1953-54 in two volumes—*The Founders* and *The Guardians.* It is at one and the same time a justification for Empire and an apologia for colonialism. In its introduction he writes, 'There comes a time in a Man's life when he may well stand back and consider what he has built, planted, written or begotten and whether it was worth doing . . . if the English look back on their history, the long connection with India will be an achievement that cannot be ignored.' This is the self-justification. Now comes the apologia, 'It is a Christian doctrine that a man must be judged not by his worst so much as by his best, and in the end not even by his best but by what he aimed at.' This would be fine, if there were agreement about what was 'aimed at' in India. Mason does not actually say so but he implies that what was aimed at was endowing India with a system of good administration, stability, civilizing institutions of judiciary and education. Mason's text is a paean to the paternalistic administration, the *Mai-baap* Raj of the ICS. Mason has raised the ICS to Platonic heights and its officers have been compared to the 'Guardians' of Plato's utopian state. This is idealistic discourse, deliberate rhetoric, in a time when the Empire had been discredited and in the process of being dismantled. In the early 1950s, when this book was first published, such discourse would have been a salve to the bruised self-image of a recently powerful nation, which was then being increasingly relegated to the sidelines of world politics by the USA and USSR.

Mason's writing is thus not only historical but in the vanguard of the first wave of Raj Nostalgia literature which began in the 1950s with the work of John Masters and H.E. Bates. The fiction of Masters and Bates exhibits the colonial stereotypes of morally superior white men—efficient and honest, dealing as best as they could with the chaos and corruption of India.[17]

The second wave of Raj Nostalgia writing came in the 1980s. In the 60s and 70s, the Raj had become a nearly forgotten, shameful relic and its prophet, Kipling, reviled for jingoism and vulgarity. This perspective changed in the 80s and both enjoyed a revival. The Raj was now a distant enough phenomenon to be viewed through the sepia-tinted glasses of nostalgia. The guilt, the shame, the disgrace belonged to another generation. For the Yuppies of Thatcher's England, the Raj provided Romantic relief from the financial constraints of a severely conservative economy. The fairy-tale quality of M.M. Kaye's *The Far Pavillions* and *The Shadow of the Moon* and even more so their slick, glossy television *avatars*, ensured their super success.[18] The vastly popular *Plain Tales from the Raj*,[19] the book form of a series of radio programmes on Raj reminiscences by aging Anglo-Indians, is yet another Raj Nostalgia volume.

For the more intellectually inclined, Paul Scott's *The Raj Quartet* provided, at one and the same time, an opportunity to purge the guilt of colonialism through its moral indictment of the Raj and to glory in what Scott and the Britons of the 80s clearly saw as the benefits of Empire. It is this element of Raj Nostalgia literature which needs to be challenged by the postcolonial order.

Distance does not lend enchantment to the Raj—at least not for the decolonized. Moreover, the high moral claims of the continuing benefits of the Raj ring hollow in the face of the threat of neo-colonialism. After all till 1857, India was ruled by a chartered commercial corporation, the

East India Company. Now in the postmodern era of multinational corporations and commercial imperialism, colonialism has come full circle. Hence the even greater need to understand colonial discourse.

The first time round, industrialized European nations had colonized pre-industrial societies and justified the act in moral and ideological terms. Now decolonized societies are once again sought to be brought under the economic and cultural hegemony of the industrialized giants. Exposure to and comprehension of colonial discourse can, by revealing the exploitative nature of colonialism, become an intellectual bulwark against the inroads of neo-colonialism.

NOTES

1. Ashcroft Bill, G. Gareth, Helen Tiffin, ed., *The Empire Writes Back: Theory and Practice in Postcolonial Literatures* (London: Routledge, 1989).
2. Even the few Indian scholars who have worked in this area, have focussed on Anglo-Indian fiction, leaving other aspects of colonial discourse untouched. See M.K. Naik, *Mirror on the Wall: Images of India and Englishman in Anglo-Indian Fiction* (1990), Sujit Bose, *Attitudes to Imperialism: Kipling, Forster and Paul Scott* (1991), Sujit Mukherjee, *Forster and Further* (1993). Although Ketaki Kushari Dyson in *Various Universe, A Study of the Journals and Memoirs of British Men and Women in the Indian Subcontinent 1765-1856* (1978), studied the letter-journals of the Anglo-Indians, she stops short at 1856 and does not take in the important 'High Raj' period. Nor has she considered imperial historical discourse.
3. See Allen J. Greenberger, *The British Images of India: A Study in the Literature of Imperialism 1880-1960* (1969), Benita Parry, *Delusions and Discoveries Studies on India in the British Imagination* (1972), Susan Howe, *Novels of Empire* (1949).
4. Edward Said, *Culture and Imperialism* (1992).
5. Edward Said, *Orientalism* (London: Routledge and Kegan, 1978).
6. Saros Cowasjee, *Women Writers of the Raj: Short Fiction from Kipling to Independence* (London: Grafton, 1990).
7. Saros Cowasjee, *Stories from the Raj: From Kipling to Independence* (1982; rep. Delhi: Indus, 1992).
8. Saros Cowasjee, *More Stories from the Raj and After: From Kipling to the Present Day* (1986; Rep. Delhi: Indus, 1992).
9. See Blunt, *Ideas about India* (1885), H.E. Bates, *The Scarlet Sword* (1950), Trevelyan Raleigh, *The Golden Oriole* (1987), George Orwell, *Burmese Days* (1934).
10. These 'sterling' qualities of the imperial representatives in India have been scathingly ridiculed by George Orwell in *Burmese Days*.

11. (London: William Heinemann, 1896).
12. (1865; Rep. Delhi: Indus, 1992).
13. (Delhi: Indus, 1991).
14. (Delhi: Indus, 1992).
15. Michael Edwardes, *British India, 1772-1947* (1967; Rep. Calcutta: Rupa, 1993), p. 149.
16. Paul Scott's quartet of Raj novels were published between 1966 and 1977; *The Jewel in the Crown, The Day of the Scorpion, Towers of Silence* and *A Division of the Spoils.*
17. See John Masters, *Bhowani Junction* (1954), *Coromandel* (1955), *The Deceivers* (1952), etc. and H.E. Bates *The Scarlet Sword.*
18. Nilufer E. Bharucha, "Raj Nostalgia Writing: Time for a Break," *The Afternoon Despatch and Courier*, 13 November 1992.
19. Charles Allen, *Plain Tales from the Raj* (Andre Deutsch, 1975).

Search for Identity in Paul Scott's *The Alien Sky* and *Staying On*, John Masters' *Bhowani Junction* and Dina Mehta's *And Some Take a Lover*

MANJUSHREE S. KUMAR

The lowering of the Union Jack at a historic moment in British-Indian history, sent a wave of thrill and elation through many a heart, saddened some, confounded others, and left quite a number realizing the inevitability and morality of this final act. The British were preparing to leave India and had handed over the country and its countrymen to self-rule. Colonialism in India was coming to an end. The English were leaving behind them not only memories of a regal and imperialistic splendour but also a net of difficult, uneasy knots in the social fabric of India. Both, during their presence in the country and after they left it, a section of people were gradually cohering into existence to form a community, which wondered and said—"Where do we belong?" They were a people for whom "Home" was neither this side, nor that side of the sea. For a large number of Indians, of distinct communities, Anglo-Indians and Eurasians, the Indian soil was *not* the native soil and the Indian sky was the Alien Sky. In an article in *New Society* Mihir Bose has examined the position of the Anglo-Indians, who, he remarks are torn between two worlds.[1] Mr. Stokoe is an Anglo-Indian who nourishes one hope, that one day he will "come home" to England. He has never seen "home" but he has tried to preserve his heritage in his room, "On a small shelf above his bed, next to a row of miniature Scotch whiskies and just above a Clark Gable photograph, there is a large Union Jack. His prized possession is the *Newsweek* cover story on the Queen's jubilee. Arlene [his wife] can barely contain herself as she speaks of England. There is a brother in the Royal Artillery, one in the Royal Marines, and all live in England." (7) British imperialism one realizes has been responsible for the creation of the "half and half." The Eurasians as they have been termed are treated with partial contempt and are held at a distance by the *pukka* Sahibs and memsahibs. An extremely poignant example of this is the predicament of Dorothy Gower and Judith Anderson in Paul Scott's *The Alien Sky*. Tom Gower, Dorothy's husband comes into the picture, as Mrs. Cynthia Mapleton mentions him as one of the "Cranks" who will be staying back even after the British leave India. Mrs. Mapleton—the harsh Britisher—sadistically speaks of the "chi-chi," the half-breeds. There is contempt in her voice and an unforgiving tone. The Eurasians have been treated "like social pariahs."[2] Both Hari Kumar in *The Jewel in the Crown* and Judith Anderson the Eurasian in *The Alien Sky* whose "skin showed dark and swarthy" (102) are victims of English sadism and an innate intolerance that bares itself as animosity. British rule had thus produced its own social hierarchy. A stratification in society accounted for the thwarted union between the Eurasians and the English or the Indians. The Anglo-Indian Victoria Jones in *Bhowani Junction* by John Masters, goes through this ordeal through the entire length of the book. Her first expression is an extremely vivid telling of the new identity:

> I've been four years among only Englishmen and Indians. Do you realize that they hardly know there is such a thing as an Anglo-Indian community? Once I heard an old English Colonel talking to an Indian—he was a young fellow, a financial adviser. The Colonel said, "What are you going to do about the Anglo-Indians, when we leave?" *"We're* not going to do anything, Colonel," the Indian said, "Their fate is in their own hands. They've just got to look around and see where they are and who they are—after you've gone."[3]

The quandary of the Anglo-Indians speaks in Victoria's assertion: "The English despise us but need us. We despise the Indians, but we need them." (26) Patrick Taylor, also a Eurasian, makes it explicit: "My God, if they [the English] leave I will go Home with them." To this, there is Victoria's rejoinder: "Home? Where is your home, man? England?" Patrick, at a deeper level of consciousness, knows that they *couldn't* go Home. He voices his predicament: "We couldn't become English, because we were half Indian. We couldn't become Indian, because we were half English. We could only stay where we were and be what we were. Here Colonel McIntyre was right too. The English would go any time now and leave us to the Wogs." (28) Victoria Jones explains her community's struggle as half-breeds, and the need to come to terms with themselves. In fact asserting themselves psychologically and proving their existence to themselves, seems to be the only way out. Mihir Bose, in his survey of the Anglo-Indian community as a creation of the postcolonial situation reflects that "their sorrow and bewilderment accurately reflect the feelings of a community which, 30 years after the British withdrawal, does not know where to turn." (7)

The Anglo-Indians, it was clear, resented the Indians and felt a hostility to Indian leadership. Rose Mary, Victoria's elder sister is enraged at the suggestion of transfer of rule to the Indians: "You talk as if you *want* the Congress to become our government!" (27) Victoria affirms the undesirability: "I don't want to see the Congress ruling here, but I am only asking you, what else is there that can happen?" (27) Shamsul Islam in *Chronicles of the Raj* presents a lucid analysis of the "plight of the Anglo-Indians on the eve of independence." He explains: "Numerically insignificant, they presented a particularly tragic problem. Midway between two cultural worlds, under the peculiar conditions of their origin and socio-cultural development, they could never really get to know the West to which they aspired to belong, nor did they have any emotional ties with India where they really belonged."[4] Colonel Rodney Savage reflects on Victoria's affiliations with himself and Ranjit. Victoria becomes engaged to Ranjit but even during the ceremony of her initiation into the Sikh fold, she realizes that a change of religion cannot alter her Anglo-Indian identity. She finally returns to Patrick: "She had always loved Patrick. They'd grown up for each other." The changes that swept across India and the world "blew through her too." "She'd tried becoming an Indian but she wasn't an Indian. She'd tried becoming English—but she wasn't English." (389) Both Victoria Jones and Patrick Taylor typify the agony of the entire Anglo-Indian community toward the end of British colonialism in India.

Paul Scott's Tusker and Lucy Smalley in *Staying On* perform a precarious, balancing act as they work out their lives in an alien ethos in the Lodge at the hill-station of Pankot. This English couple had decided to stay on, and this they do through the sap of nostalgia. Though they have been spared the ordeal of emerging as the half and half, they live in a condition of rootlessness. Home, for them too, is a distant proposition. Stripped of their erstwhile dignity, they live a life that is a shabby, even a wretched, one. Mrs. Lucy Smalley remarks on the dress that she is wearing as the only decent one that she possesses and the only moment of luxury for her are the occasional meals of chicken pilao or gin and lime juice at the hotel. Efforts to sustain their sagging spirits marks the poignance of their situation. For them, as ones who have chosen to stay back, there is a reversal of roles. These last of the English find themselves low down in the post-independence Indian social hierarchy. They are still aliens in a country whose people will not absorb them in their social system. Lucy's conscious but untiring efforts to work out a decent living for herself and her husband is a pathetic preamble to the desolation and homelessness that is in store for her. She would have to live amid the "alien corn"[5] with no one of her kind to comfort her. With the British having left India, not only is their claim for superiority annulled, they are even denied the chance to survive as respectable citizens in what they think is now their home.

It is pathetic that the English officer Tusker Smalley and his wife are compelled to depend (rather than be depended on) on the unscrupulous Mrs. Bhoolabhoy the proprietress of Smith's Hotel and the annexe, and Ibrahim their servant. It is only the latter who recognizes them as Sahib and memsahib. Their identities have become hazy and need desperately to be clung to. Their existence in effect, grows into a cocoon's that admits Ibrahim, their only servant, the Eurasian hair dresser, the Indian clergy in the church, and a couple of Indian friends. The frequent skirmishes between Lucy and her husband Tusker point to what they are trying to preserve as the Sahib and memsahib. Having to undergo humiliation is much more painful to Lucy, but she accepts her condition with a mild stoicism.

Indians like Mrs. Bhoolabhoy wait with a vengeance to overpower and dislodge the Smalleys. Her proposal to ask them to move into the new hotel, the "Shiraz" is backed by her fury and reproachful words: "What they can afford or not afford does not interest me. It is no concern of mine. When *they* ruled the roost *our* concerns did not enter their heads. It is tit for tat." (193) Homelessness and a subsequent helplessness is exasperating for Lucy Smalley and there is a note of sorrow and pain at her being alone and "having to rely for human sympathy and moral support upon people who frankly do not care for me, not deeply." and for whom Lucy did not "deeply care either." (103) She had to cope with an intractable, obstinate husband, a destitute present and a future in which she sees desertion and loneliness. An existence in colonial India and later a life in the postcolonial times was apparently a disturbed one for many who could not discover or decipher their positions in the social structure.

We come across a striking parallel of a non-belongingness, in Dina Mehta's most recent novel *And Some Take a Lover.* The period is the turmoil and turbulence of the pre-independence movement in India. I discovered that this note of an unconnectedness, if I may so phrase it, among the Parsees in India, at this period, is rather dominant in this novel and stands out as a component of the context in which the lives and movements of Roshni and others of her community are worked out. It is the comment made by Rustom at the beginning of the novel that introduces the issue of their rootlessness. It is his remark at the gathering at his party: "Did you not feel how rootless they are? That they do not belong? What has this country to offer us? What kind of cultural life? We Parsees are aliens here. And our days are numbered after the British leave."[6] Roshni is quick to question: "Where, then, do we belong?" The answer that Rustom offers brings back to our minds the Anglo-Indian affinity for the English. Rustom is emphatic and convinced. "I know where I belong. I was educated in England. I lived there four years. Then I went back and completed two years at the Manchester University. They are a wonderful people. I wish I could impress on you how rich life there can be." (19) This glorification of the English, whom he is now distanced from, is followed by denigrating remarks about his immediate milieu: "Isn't there much that is crassly materialistic in the Indian culture?" He has evidently drifted away from the national mainstream. He continues: "What about our stark contrasts of poverty and wealth? The communal and class conflicts? Our lack of a social conscience?" (19) It is impossible for him to think of his roots in a milieu he so vehemently despises. Roshni, though, in the course of the narrative appears to espouse the national cause, had, at this moment of her conversation with Rustom, felt just as uprooted, even dissociated: "He is like me, she thought, in that he feels he does not belong here. But while I feel like mere driftwood caught up in the swirl of these past two years, he stupidly believes he can come to shore *there;* and I belong nowhere." (19)

The story of her predicament has only begun to develop. Her friendship and attraction for Sudhir Mahipal, an Indian and a Hindu, turns her and her inclination for the exclusively Indian stream of living which included wearing the Khadi, an involvement in the campaigns led by Mahatma Gandhi, and an inculcation of the philosophy and thinking of the Indian leader. But this meets with strict opposition by her mother who thinks it is atrocious. "That we should allow our girls to marry outside the community, mate with *parjat?*" (37) Roshni's aunt Pirojakaki is equally severe as she denounces the community outside her own, and the Indian leadership: "how could Roshni be rapturous over a Hindu? How could she mix with people of other communities, wear clothes that made her look like a gunny sack, raise slogans about Independence and 'Quit India' and follow in the footsteps of the scoundrel and vagrant, Mohandas Karamchand Gandhi, who went about bare down to his navel?" (38) Once again there are echoes of confused identities, echoes of what one has heard from Victoria Jones, and Rose Mary in *Bhowani Junction*. The painful struggle to establish one's identity goes on and "In Pirojabai's home M.K. had been the arch-traitor, the unmentionable, except with abuse, but a large portrait of George VI had adorned the wall over her bed and she felt a burning sense of loyalty towards her king. How could the rule of so handsome a man not be just and benevolent? No, the nationalists were wrong, *juthu boul*—why tell lies?" (38)

There is a subtle presentation of another version of non-belongingness here, in the specific context of Roshni's life. She has received a western education and has a life style that is more English than Indian. However, she feels she can commit herself to the task Sudhir had set for himself. But Sudhir evidently thinks otherwise, and in one of their meetings, discloses rather harshly, but truthfully, that Roshni wore khadi to assume a role "complete with costume and dialogue" and that she deceived none other but herself. In this exchange charged with emotion, Sudhir impresses on her, with a vehemence that she ought to be herself. Infuriated and agonized, she lashes back "You want me to be myself! . . . And what am I, for God's sake?" (170) An identity is being cross-questioned, and for the rest of the book, we watch Roshni struggling with herself, with her association with friends, and with incidents that spell certain intrigues. She is living under a perpetual strain which comes in the wake of her struggle to find herself. Her liaison with a wide range of people storms her life and there is a kind of a liberation that she seeks for herself.

The pattern one discerns in Dina Mehta's novel is a mosaic that fits into itself lives and ways of the Parsee community, the focus being on Roshni, her family and friends, the emotional struggle of Roshni and Sudhir and how events marking the independence struggle shape the lives and destinies of the twin protagonists. She is, till the end, "the in-between, the half-way person.' (316) But here and now she must begin. Victoria Jones, Judith Anderson and Dorothy Gower, Lucy Smalley and Roshni, must all unmask and bring themselves to the brink of their identities. The search must go on.

NOTES

1. Mihir Bose, "One Corner of an Indian slum that is forever England," *New Society*, 4 Jan. 1979, pp. 7-9.
2. Paul Scott, *The Alien Sky* (London: Grafton, 1974), p. 27.
3. John Masters, *Bhowani Junction* (London: Sphere, 1954), p. 26.
4. Shamsul Islam, *Chronicles of the Raj* (London: Macmillan, 1979), p. 97.
5. Paul Scott, *Staying On* (London: Granada, 1978), p. 105.
6. Dina Mehta, *And Some Take a Lover* (Calcutta: Rupa, 1992), p. 18.

Re-reading Joyce Cary's *Mister Johnson*: A Postcolonial Perspective

VINITA BHATNAGAR

Many factors have been conventionally held responsible for the growth of the novelistic genre—the growth of the bourgeoise, the rise of democracy and the spread of print capitalism. In his book *Culture and Imperialism*[1] Said locates the roots of the novelistic genre in the growth of imperialism. Thus he sees it as no coincidence that the novel is inaugrated in England by *Robinson Crusoe*, a work whose protagonist is the founder of a new world, which he rules and reclaims for Christianity and England. *Robinson Crusoe* is clearly enabled by an ideology of overseas expansion. Later novelists situate their work in and derive it from a carefully surveyed territorial greater Britain.

This link between the genre, its place of origin and its implicit political ideology makes its import into imperialized locations an interesting area of exploration. Through the course of this paper, an attempt will be made to discuss the ways in which colonial novelists negotiate with generic expectations of the classic realist novel as being concerned with the story of individuals and with the historical reality of a colonial setting that reduces the colonial masters in such a way that they can no longer be seen as individuals but must share a collective identity as colonial bureaucrats. The text taken for analysis is Joyce Cary's *Mister Johnson*[2] which tries to resolve this intrinsic contradiction.

Set in colonial Nigeria, *Mister Johnson* is a text attacked in this postcolonial era for its stereotypical depiction of Nigeria and its inhabitants. Its author, an English official of Irish birth, writing within the traditions of a culture and a political system which sought to justify colonialism either as it were or as reformers thought it should be, shared the large formation of European attitudes and practice towards Africa, out of which emerged what late twentieth century critics have called Africanism or Africanist discourse. Thus Cary writes of the Africans in terms that define their non-adult status, the warm-heartedness of the African, his readiness for friendship on the smallest encouragement and his fickleness.

Cary's choice of the present tense, chosen because he conceived of Johnson as living in the present, "from hour to hour" and his vision of a static and unchanging Africa impelled Achebe, in 1964,[3] to retell Cary's story from the Nigerian point of view in *Arrow of God*. Achebe's reaction to Cary's novel is well documented and will not be repeated here. Nor will the familiar and truthful allegations of stereotypical depiction be rehearsed once more. What this paper intends is to explore the ways in which *Mister Johnson* constructs the colonizing subject in ways that highlight the complexity of the subject, the difficulties that the subject encounters in the process of colonization and the struggle for a new identity in an alien context.

This is done through the story of Rudbeck, Junior bureaucrat in the colonial administrative service of Nigeria. The novel traces his growth from the stage of total surrender to the bureaucratic mechanism to a stage of moral pathos where he is celebrated in the dying thoughts of Johnson for "greatness," goodness and daring inventiveness. At the end of the novel Rudbeck manages to transcend the alienation implicit in the lives of colonial master in exile from their mother country by asserting the primacy of human relations against the codified rules that govern bureaucracy.[4]

Colonial experience is thus presented as a process of self-endangering and self-renewal and serves as a rite of passage towards total manhood. When Rudbeck begins colonial service he is European in dress, tools, modes of travel and thought. He is posted to Fada, a pioneer settlement five or six hundred years old, built on its own rubbish heaps, without charm even of antiquity. Its squalor and its stints are all new. But the hideousness of this picture constiture the very subjectivity of the colonizing subject and separates the colonizers from those who would never leave the comforts of their homes.

The would-be colonizer, the person defined by European technologies and habits of mind becomes through a dynamogenic process the 'colonizing subject.' Questions of the subjectivity of the colonizer have been elided in recent postcolonial theory so that colonization is invariably seen as an encounter between the 'Mechanism' or 'impersonal system' which is the colonial power and the colonized, who are increasingly seen as a heterogeneous group. Such a reading grossly simplifies the identity of the colonizing subject as this analysis of *Mr. Johnson* should reveal.

Rudbeck is first presented to us as an eager young bureaucrat who learns the facial mannerism and fetches of his seniors and mirrors them faithfully. He pokes his head forward and utters loud exclamations like his first D.O., Sturdee; and he sits at his office table, with his chin in the air and his eyelids cast down, like Blore.

Within the type of the impassive, automatized bureaucrat, there are sub-types available. This is most clearly apparent in their differing reactions to the building of a road in Fada. Thus Blore considers motor roads to be the ruin of Africa "bringing swindlers, thieves and whores, disease, vice and corruption, and the vulgarities of trade, among decent unspelt tribesmen."

Tring represents another sub-type of the colonial bureaucrat—that of the ambitious, overzealous bureaucrat who will be chief secretary one day. Tring has assented to the process of mechanization whereby spontaneous, natural impulses are repressed in the interests of a supposed objectivity. It is in contrast to these characters that Cary portrays Rudbeck as reacting with moral outrage to the service conditions that make dehumanization of the bureaucrat possible.

This outrage initially takes the form of a subtle subversion where Rudbeck manipulates words and figures in the ledgers and files in order to make more money available for road building. Significantly it is Johnson who gives him this suggestion as it is Johnson who facilitates the process of hiring labourers, embezzling money and settling deadlines. This leads to Rudbeck's awareness of Johnson's role as more than an operative tool for building the road: "He's the man with the ideas," Rudbeck says, and then with added perception, "In fact, if it wasn't for him and Tasuki there wouldn't be a road even up this far."

Rudbeck's obsession with the making of roads started with his training under Sturdee. His motivation for making the roads stemmed from a Messianic self-perception and a belief in the benevolence of colonial rule. To build the road meant to increase trade and to break tribal isolation. But unexpected and unwanted results negate his achievement. This leaves Rudbeck looking at the ruins of a society he set out to help. Under his innocent hand "things fall apart." Rudbeck begins to feel used and driven like a blind instrument by the entire machinery of colonialism that brings in its wake, bureaucracy and the reduction of individuals to mere automatons. While in the earlier part of his career Rudbeck had accepted the frustrating and alienating nature of his service by cheerfully asserting "Ours not to reason why" he is now unable to find that blind obedience within himself.

Events move towards a crisis as Johnson is implicated for the murder of Gollup. Rudbeck's refusal to accept Butleel's offer of assistance is the first symptom of his new reaction to the conditions of his service. In a steadily accelerating process of rebellion he turns himself into a robot who submits gracefully and carries out instructions to the letter in order to make a mockery of them. By overemphasizing the formality and the correctness of his responses, Rudbeck parodies the dehumanizing effects of his service. In delaying the execution of the warrant, in attempting to coach Johnson in the correct responses during the trial and in finally transgressing against codified rules that limit his life by shooting Johnson himself, Rudbeck defies the system that would deny him moral choices.

In the process he achieves what Mahood calls his "imaginative liberation," the realization that Johnson is not absurd or dangerous or pathetic or anything else but gifted with the mastery to shape his own life and even to shape its close. The narrative moves towards this inevitable conclusion and obstacles presented by the appearance of a wife, Celia's illness, their subsequent transfer and the reprimand by the head office for the irregularities regarding funds merely serve to draw out the process.

There are significant areas of silencing within the text especially in reference to all forms of internal organized resistance to colonialism. An oppositional reading of the text would thus emphasize the ways in which *Mister Johnson* conforms to what Said described as a Western style for dominating, restructuring and having authority on the Orient.[5] Critics like Homi Bhabha, Abdul Jan Mohammed and Gayatri Spivak have sought to offer ways of dismantling colonialism's signifying systems and exposing its operation in the silencing and oppressing of the colonized subject.

The silence of the text revolves around the story and history of the non-white inhabitants of Nigeria who occupy the "other" side of colonial divide. Not just as the petty clerks who work for the government but the sullen, silent majority who live in small hamlets and villages and view the white invaders with suspicion and distrust.

It was precisely this story that Achebe set out to tell. His decision to retell Cary's story "from the inside" was triggered by the superficiality of Cary's representation of Nigeria and the stereotypical depiction of Nigerian characters. Achebe's decision to retell Cary's story had implications only partially suggested by the contrast between a "most superficial picture" and a "look from the inside." Cary was not merely an outsider observing Nigeria in a disinterested manner; his view was scarcely an objective one. He came to Nigeria as a colonial administrator and his novel can be located within the long line of novels written by colonial administrators, or those employing a colonial backdrop. In keen incisive critiques of such novels Said reveals[4] the way in which the narrative strategies of these works function to maintain the established order of an Imperial England at the centre and a series of overseas territories connected to it at the peripheries.

The continuity of British Imperial policy throughout the nineteenth century—in fact a narrative—is actively accompanied by this novelistic process, whose main purpose is not to raise more questions, not to disturb or otherwise preoccupy attention, but to keep the empire more or less in place.

The ability to place Cary's *Mister Johnson* within such a canon of novels and the understanding of the historical location of the text as written by a colonial administrator in colonized Nigeria does not excuse the text's wilfull blindness to the lived experience of the colonized subjects.

And yet, there are ways in which this text can be read as innovative in its exploration and analysis of the subjectivity of the colonial subject. The autobiographical element in the text finds a resonance in Rudbeck's anguished questioning of his position as administrator in Nigeria. It is in exploring the internal contradictions and complexities of the resources of authority, and in analyzing the ways in which the act of becoming a colonizing subject could be read as an act of self-regeneration that Cary depicts the ideals and fantasies generated in the metropolitan centres of empire, which made colonialism possible. For this reason, if only for this reason, Cary should be included in any corpus of literature centered around colonial discourse.

NOTES

1. Edward Said, *Culture and Imperialism* (London: Verso).
2. Joyce Cary, born in Londonderry, Northern Ireland, joined the Nigerian Political Service, 1913; Magistrate and Executive Officer 1913-1920; Recipient Black Memorial Prize. *Mister Johnson* was published in 1939.
3. Chinua Achebe, born in Ogidi, East Central State, published four novels between 1958 and 1966 before turning to short stories and poetry. In *Arrow of God* Achebe returns to the past, this time to the 1920s when Nigerian tribal life had to accommodate itself to the colonial administration. Both Ezeulu, the tribal priest, and Winterbottom, the colonial administrator fail because they try to impose their own rigid deterministic philosophy on an intransigent world. T.J. Winnifrith, *Great Writers of the English Language Novelists and Prose Writers,* ed. James Vision (London and Basingstoke: The Macmillan Press, 1979), p. 11.
4. A. Norman Jeffares biographical note on Cary sums up *Mister Johnson* in these words: Mister Johnson, ultimately a tragicomedy, is the best of the

African novels, where the difference of values between the administrator Rudbeck, and his exuberant, devoted servant, Mr. Johnson, has a tragic outcome. Mr. Johnson bound remorselessly to the circle of fortune's wheel. . . . These novels are not designed to exhibit Africa, to examine colonialism; it is true they have an exhilaration, a violence, a touch of the fabulous, but Cary's concern is with some of the fundamentals of human behaviour. He sets the novels in the Africa he saw in his particular idiosyncratic way because he was there, because he saw there at first hand tensions between tribal and Western society, and because his interpretation of Africa permitted him a dramatic setting and themes for his examination of human beings in unreal situations.

Colonial and Postcolonial Images of Indonesia in Dutch, British and Australian Literature from 1618 to 1992

DAVID MYERS

It is fascinating, not just in literary terms, but also in socio-political terms, to trace the changes in European images of Indonesia from the adventurous and exotic voyage of Captain Bontokoe in 1618 to the moral revolt against colonial exploitation mounted by Multatuli (John Douves Dekkers) in his novel *Max Havelaar or the Coffee Auctions of the Dutch Trading Company* in 1860. The pattern of European reactions to Java, Sumatra, Borneo and Malaya becomes more psychologically complex with such novels and stories as Joseph Conrad's *Almayer's Folly* and *The Rescue* and Somerset Maugham's Borneo stories such as "The Outstation."

Even with Conrad and Maugham there is still no real conviction that the sun is about to set on the British and Dutch colonial empires in Malaya and Indonesia. On the contrary. The most that one can say is that the authors' universal humanism and genuine sympathy and admiration for the indigenous inhabitants of the East Indies are balanced against the implicit assumption that superior European technology and weaponry will continue to found empires in the southern hemisphere.

Some authors such as Lousi Couperus in *The Hidden Force* in 1899[2] show in their fiction how the rich cultures of the Dutch East Indies infiltrate the European souls of the colonial administrators and change them for ever, so that many are no longer at home in Europe but are not yet accepted in their equatorial home. They become deracinated, cross-cultural "Indisch" people.

It is not really until the 1930s that European fiction begins to build on *Max Havelaar*'s excoriating satire on colonialism in emerging Indonesia. It has been said that history is no more and no less than the propaganda lies of the victors and this may have been true of most European history and fiction about the Dutch East Indies until the

1930s. Certainly it is no longer images of upper class Europeans coping with the administration of the tropical colonies that preoccupy the writers, but rather a revisionist history of what constitutes heroism and what constitutes human rights and of course also a reconsideration of the vital evaluative question: on which side of the battle lines were the heroes and on which side were the savages to be found? Vicki Baum's *Tale of Bali* in 1937 fits this category and so too do Madelon Lulofs' novels *Rubber* and *Coolie*.

Soldiers of the Allied Army in World War II witness the dissolution of the British and Dutch Empires and find new attitudes to the Indonesians in the course of the Allied war against the new Japanese Empire. These war-reminiscences included Jon Clery's *The Long Pursuit* (1967), Robert Macklin's *The Paper Castle* (1977) and Dirk Bogarde's *A Gentle Occupation* (1980).

There are at least seven recent Australian novels which show how new myths of national identity may now be formed out of the tragic clash between Australian and the culturally alien nations of the Asia-Pacific. These novel are Randolph Stow's *The Visitants*, Thea Astley's *Beachmasters*, Robert Drewe's *Cry in the Jungle Bar*, Blanche d'Alpuget's *Turtle Beach*, Christopher Koch's *The Year of Living Dangerously*, Timothy Mo's *The Redundancy of Courage* and Lee's *Troppo Man*.

Entirely new themes for Australian literature now emerge. Instead of studying nineteenth century European novels which often feature the cultural arrogance and assumptions of religious superiority made by European colonial administrators, we now find Australian sometimes stoic and sometimes impish anti-heroes venturing with naively and confusion into the maelstrom of South East Asian politics.

By contrast, the Australian mass media delight in maintaining assumptions of superiority and condescension towards South East Asia, based on our multi-party democracy, our allegedly fair distribution of wealth and justice and our alleged lack of corruption. Australian media have tended to condescend to South East Asia on the grounds of government corruption and big business corruption, arbitrary dictatorship or rule by military junta, overpopulation and widespread poverty, uncontrollable crime and violence rates and the inability of countries in South East Asia to find stability, equity, and civilized discourse without violence.

It is an ironic footnote on this hobby of the Australian media that in the last few years since the 1980s boom and bust, there have been more than enough stories within Australia of corruption and incompetence in state governments and big business. The final poetic irony about the

Australian attempt to adopt a superior attitude to Asia is over belated realization that we are well on the way to becoming an economic colony of another Asian nation, Japan, for whom we are little more than a mineral quarry and a tourism destination.

Let us now, however, begin at the beginning, with Captain Bontekoe's *Journalen van de Gedenkcwaerdige Reisen van Willem Ijsbrandtszoon Bontekoe* (1618-1625).[4] The amusing thing about these diary-journals is the combination of exotic adventure, deadly disaster and the constant appeals to God's allegedly all-merciful hand. Captain Bontekoe's ship catches fire, ignites the gunpowder and blows them sky high. Captain Bontekoe's reaction is to raise his arms to heaven and shout "Here I go, O Lord! Have mercy upon your sinner." (*Insulinde*, 6) After twelve days at sea in a longboat they happen upon land in the Dutch East Indies and Captain Bontekoe falls on his knees and thanks God for his grace and mercy because the crew had resolved that on the next day they would take the boys and eat them. Captain Bontekoe leads a mission upstream to purchase a buffalo for five and a half pieces of eight (10) and bellows loud hymns in order to appear brave and unafraid when the head-hunting villagers of Sumatra seem determined to slit his throat with their kris. These and other blood-thirsty adventures assail Captain Bontekoe and every time that he survives by the skin of his teeth, no matter how many other godless corpses there are who were less lucky than he, he thanks the Lord for His kindness, and marvels at this "remarkable sign of God's providence." (16)

Translator and editor Cornelia N. Moore comments thus: "Travel narratives like these, hastily printed and cheaply edited, full of mishaps, shipwrecks, deserted islands, 'savages,' exotic continents and tropical climates gave the well dressed Dutchman behind his potbelly stove a window to horizons wider than even his flat country could provide. It also gave him a taste of the glorious role the Dutch were playing in the world. That these voyagers might be trampling upon the liberty of others did not occur to proud Dutch, who themselves had just wrestled independence from the Spanish Habsburgs and the Holy Roman Empire." (3)

One hundred and fifty years later between 1768 and 1778 Captain Johan Splinter Stavorinus of the V.O.C. undertook several voyages for the Far East Indian Company. He is less concerned with bloodthirsty accounts of adventures with savages than he is with moral and racist judgments on the inhabitants of the Dutch colonies, for example: "Insomuch as the women of the Indies are by no means devoid of intelligence, they could become useful members of society if only they were kept from continual contact with slaves and were brought up under the supervision of parents who deemed it a duty to instill in them, from a tender age, the principles of morality and good behaviour. . . . As soon as a child is born, it is turned over to the care of female slaves, who normally suckle it and rear it until it reaches the age of nine or ten. These slaves often have little more intellect than an animal, and the children acquire all their bad habits, prejudices and superstitions—which stay with them for the rest of their lives. It is not surprising that they turn out to be more like their despised slaves than the offspring of noble parents." (22)

There is a gap of another one hundred years to the epoch-making novel of John Dekker, *Max Havelaar or the Coffee Auctions of the Dutch Trading Company* written in 1860. During this time the Dutch had established themselves as conquerors in the Dutch East Indies and had set up a well-organized colonial administration with which to exploit the natural resources and the human resources, particularly of the island of Java.

Dekker published his masterpiece under the pen-name of Multatuli ("I have suffered much") because it was based on his own dismissal from the Dutch colonial civil service after he had tried unsuccessfully to urge major reforms in Dutch treatment of the Javanese peasants. *Max Havelaar* is a sometimes impassioned and sometimes sarcastic satire on the complacency of the Dutch burghers and administrators who, by the nineteenth century, had turned rural Java into a kind of fascist indentured-labour colony. *Max Havelaar* exposes the collaboration of the Dutch administrators with the Javanese aristocracy to oppress the Javanese peasants with forced labour on coffee or rubber plantations, or kultuuurstelsel as it was called. It is interesting that Pramoedya Ananta Toer's narrator in *Awakenings*, Minke, takes up this identical theme in a highly emotional revolt against both the tyrannical Dutch and also against his own father, a Javanese aristocrat or bupati. It is small wonder that the ideology of communism should find fertile ground in this society.

The anthology *Insulinde* includes two very different examples from *Max Havelaar, The Sermon of the Reverend Blatherer* and *The Story of Saijah and Adinda*. Both are extremely well-written and in quite different styles. Batavous Drystubble (Droogstoppel), who is a parody of a Dutch coffee-merchant, write *The Sermon of the Reverend Blatherer* in the first person and is allowed to satirize his own immeasurable greed. He inadequately disguises his own greed through a rhetorical veneer of missionary zeal and self-righteousness and the result is a devastating satire of religious hypocrisy that is reminiscent of Mark Twain's famous satires on what we might call religious imperialism during the opium-wars in China in his two pieces *To the Person Sitting in Darkness* and *The War Prayer*.

Self-righteous Batavus Drystubble excoriates the reformist manuscript of Max Havelaar which has fallen into his hands by accident as "Scarfman's pestilential parcel." Mr. Drystubble equates religious sanctimony with bourgeois respectability and the proof that you have found God's grace is the successful amassing of bourgeois wealth. Conversely, if you are poor, this means that you have been irreligious. Scarfman— and the name is only a thin disguise for the reformer and outspoken critic of the Dutch colonial administration, Max Havelaar himself, because he has no overcoat but only a scarf to protect him from the cold of the Dutch winter—has been "unseemly" and therefore the Lord has rightly punished him with poverty. Scarfman's unseemliness consists in his having offended against the bourgeois code of not rocking the boat, the boat that brings in the coffee and spices, grown by forced coolie labour, from the East Indies to Holland. He has rocked the boat by daring to criticize the morality of the Dutch colonial system.

Scarfman has proven that coffee cannot be grown in the region of Lebak. Drystubble's response is that they must therefore either change the soil or shift the Javanese peasants to a part of the country that is suitable for growing coffee. The self-righteousness and exaggerated posture of his ravings are only a reduction ad absurdum of the historically real exploitation of Javanese peasants under the forced labour or indirect taxation system of kultuurelstel. The author cleverly varies the tone. It begins with light-hearted farce when Drystubble admonishes his son for chasing girls instead of devoting himself to being respectable, that is, to being pious in public and making money. But it concludes with some deadly serious sarcasm about religious bigotry and hypocrisy by taking excerpts from the Reverend Blatherer's sermon.

The Reverned Blatherer refers to the Indonesian Archipelago as "the loathsome snakepits of heathenish ignorance" and refers to the prophet Mohammed as "a false prophet who is an abomination in the sight of the Lord." (*Insulinde*, 30) The Javanese must be converted immediately to Christianity by the Dutch Missionary Society. Blatherer sets out to prove "the love of God" but really evokes the "God of righteous retribution." (31) His evocation of eternal suffering in Gehenna culminates in his vision of the punishment of the un-Christian Javanese: "See how the black skin is stripped from the unbaptized child that, scarce born, was flung away from the breast of the woman into the pool of everlasting damnation." (31)

Finally the Reverned Blatherer reveals the real reason why the Dutch are in the East Indies, which of course has nothing to do with money:

"The ships of our Holland sail the great waters, to bring civilization, religion, Christianity, to the misguided Javanese! Nay, our happy Fatherland does not covet eternal bliss for itself alone: we wish to share it also with the wretched creatures on those distant shores who lie bound in the fetters of unbelief, superstition and immorality!" (31)

This is one of the most brilliant satires on the hypocrisy of colonialism that I have ever read. It has far more emotional impact than the most erudite, economic histories that painstakingly prove the Dutch exploitation of the Javanese because it has shown the role of religion in this equation and exposed the way in which Europe covered indecent greed with unbelievable piety.

Then in a passage that seems to be a sharp parody of Max Weber's theory of the Protestant work ethic, Mr. Drystubble manages somehow to prove that by forcing the Javanese to work as coolies on the coffee plantations, the Dutch are magnaminously helping the Javanese to find salvation through hard work: "So isn't it our duty to bring these people salvation? And when, as a means thereto, labour is necessary—I myself have labored on 'Change for twenty years'—may we then refuse labour to the Javanese, knowing that his soul is so urgently in need of it to escape the everlasting fire hereafter? It would be selfishness, abonimable selfishness, if we didn't make every effort to preserve those poor lost sheep from the terrible future Parson Blatherer so eloquently described." (33)

The moving tale of Saijah and Adinda is narrated in a completely different tone which possibly crosses the line from empathy to sentimentality. It is a story about Javanese peasants told from a Javanese point of view and in this respect must have broken new ground, as most colonial literature focused on the Dutch colonialists and their point of view on the difficulties of administering the territory of the East Indies.

Saijah's father falls into poverty and desperation because the Javanese regent, who is just as arbitrary and as ruthless as the Dutch administrators, takes away his water buffalo in order to kill it and eat it. This leaves Saijah's father with no way to slough his rice paddy and no way to pay his land tax. But if he doesn't pay it, he knows that he will be thrown into gaol. After he has used up his life savings to buy new water buffaloes, he gives up and tries to run away. The Dutch have him shipped for trying to run away and throw him in prison where he dies.

Saijah, who is chastely and loyally in love with the maiden Adinda, leaves for thrice twelve moons to seek his fortune as a houseboy in Batavia, so that he can amass enough capital to buy a water buffalo and marry Adinda. But just before he returns to claim her, Adinda's father, who has also had his water buffalo stolen by the regent, flees to join the rebels on a remote island in the Lampong Districts. Saijah pursues them and eventually discovers the mutilated bodies of his beloved Adinda and her family who have been raped and killed by the Dutch army in yet another heroic battle. Saijah flings himself unarmed against the Dutch sword-bayonets to seek the merciful release of death. The Dutch celebrate a great victory over the heathen with thanksgiving services to God and with medals for heroism.

Once again the author Multatuli has proven that art and literature are much more powerful than history or sociology in evoking horrifying images of the colonized Dutch East Indies. The author goes on in a very overly didactic coda to draw the historical lessons that must be drawn from his "romantic" story. He says: "And to others, who will perhaps contend that I have idealized Saijah and his love, I must put the question: 'How do you know?' For it is a fact that very few Europeans think it worth their trouble to stoop and observe the emotions of those coffee- and sugar-making machines we call 'natives.'" (*Insulinde*, 53)

I think that it is now quite clear how this lecture on foreign images of the East Indies or Indonesia is intended as a companion-piece or counterpart to the images of Indonesia which are evoked by Indonesia's two most prominent, contemporary literary figures, Pramoedya Ananta Toer and Mochtar Lubis. Pramoedya Toer and Mochtar Lubis are inevitably concerned, each in his own different way, with passionate and tragic images of Indonesia's historical struggle for independence and with their commitments to contrasting paths for the achievement of economic and political maturity for Indonesia. Incidentally, Mochtar Lubis said about such Dutch authors as Multatuli, Couperus and Du Perron: "When these Dutch writers wrote about Indonesians, they tended to romanticize them, or they wrote about the mysterious facets of Indonesian life, which they barely understood or knew."[6]

Louis Couperus' novel, *The Hidden Force* (1899), for example, shows the ironically insidious way in which the legends and spirits of Indonesia could avenge themselves on the rational, scientific Dutch administrators. Van Oudjik is the Dutch resident in a rural part of Java where he requires the cooperation and support of the aristocratic Javanese Regents, the Adinigrats. When his European notions of efficiency and public service dictate that he should sack a member of the Adiningrat family, he incurs their wrath which is expressed indirectly through supernatural forces. The ghostly moaning of little children's voices is heard in the night and glasses mysteriously shatter without reason. But the climax occurs when van Oudjik's second wife, Leonie, who is having an adulterous affair with Oudjik's self-indulgent son, Theo, is besmirched and befouled by demons spitting betel juice all over her once pure white body. This may sound rather funny to our ears, but it is an event that is evoked with eerie atmosphere and horror a la Edgar Allan Poe by Louis Couperus.

There is of course not only an Indonesian superstitious aspect to this story, there is also a moralizing, European aspect. Van Oudjik is deceived by his entire family and finally deserted by them, when they flee in guilt before these supernatural happenings. Van Oudjik earns the narrator's praise by sticking it out alone, but in the end he pays a heavy price. He repels the "hidden force" of the foul demons in the haunted house of the residency, but he is a shaken man in his soul and subsequently resigns because he has never been able to understand these "hidden forces," just as he has never realized how deceitfully his own family had betrayed him. In the end the mysterious transcendence of Indonesian monsters and demons has its triumph. As James Rush comments: "In Couperus' Java, the Dutch may exercise civil authority, but the forces of Indonesian life, and not simply the 'hidden forces,' possess a transcendent power all their own."

Inevitably most Dutch and British fiction about the East Indies focus on points of contact and conflict between colonial administrator and often mutinous Malays or Javanese. Somerset Maugham in his fine story "The Outstation" shows how tactful and understanding the British administrators in remote jungle areas needed to be if they were to retain the loyalty and helpful support of their servants and subjects. His character portraits of the upper middle class snob, Warburton, who has been called George by the Prince of Wales, and his egalitarian assistant in the Borneo jungle, Cooper, a colonial from Barbados who envies and resents all English public school boys, offer a fine study in contrast for post-World War I English society. But paradoxically it is the snob Warburton who has infinite tact and diplomacy with the Malays and the Dayaks. It is said that "with the Malays he had a happy mixture of condescension and kindliness." This psychological extension of his English snobbism to Borneo is explained by Somerset Maugham with these words:

> The position he [the snob Warburton] found himself in flattered his vanity; he was no longer the sycophant craving the smiles of the great, he was the master whose word was law. He was gratified by the guard of Dayak soldiers who presented arms as he passed. He liked to sit in judgement on his fellow man. It pleased him to compose quarrels between rival chiefs. . . . And little by little he conceived a deep love for the Malays. . . .
>
> "In my day," he would say, "I have been on intimate terms with

> some of the greatest gentlemen in England, but I have never known finer gentlemen than some well-born Malays whom I am proud to call my friends."[8]

By contrast the pseudo-democrat Cooper is brutal and arrogant with his Malay servants, who leave him at the first opportunity. He has brought overt racism with him from Barbados and he refers to the Malays repeatedly as "niggers." Cooper is warned by his superior officer, Warburton, that he is putting his life at risk. But really Warburton loathes his junior officer, who has mocked him as a snob, and he can't wait until the inevitable disaster happens to Cooper. After Cooper's handsome Malay servant is insulted one time too many, he runs amok with his kris and murders the British administrator. Warburton ironically views Cooper's corpse, removes the kris, and affably explains that after the murderer has served a year of two of gaol sentence, he will accept him into his household and train him as a servant.

In his Preface to his Malaysian short stories, *Ah King*, Somerset Maugham wrote:

> In none of my stories of this kind have I made any attempt to deal with the natives of the countries which are their scene except in so far as they affect the white men who live among them. It is hard enough for an English writer to know anything about his own countrymen, whom he knows after all not only by observation, but by feeling, habit and knowledge of himself; . . . When it comes to members of another race I doubt whether he can know anything at all. The motives of the brown man and the yellow are written in a code of which the white man does not possess the key. . . . Some writers have given portraits of Indians and Chinese which have verisimilitude; I cannot help asking myself whether they seem so lifelike for any other reason than that they are conventional.

But in the 1930s author Vicki Baum was able in a sense to go beyond these self-set limitations of Somerset Maugham and to give a very persuasive depiction not only of the customs of the Balinese aristocracy and the Balinese peasants, but also to some degree of their motivations and ambitions. In all fairness to Maugham, it should be noted that he aimed at writing stories showing an intimately understood crisis in a white administrator's soul and he did this well, while at the same time showing the relevance of the colonial tropics to the crisis.

In *A Tale from Bali*, 1930 (originally *Das Ende des Anfangs*), Vicki Baum differentiates well between liberal, sympathetic Dutch rulers in

Bali in 1904 and jingoistic, autocratic administrators who wish to rule the East Indies by bloodshed and fear. As her sympathies are markedly with the Balinese people, Baum's depiction of the Dutch administrators is ironic, if not mildly satirical. Take this passage:

> Cannon were better than concessions, Boomsmer considered. He had a ticklish sense of honour and in his opinion the Dutch government was too easy-going. The mere mention of Bali made them all grow sentimental, he thought irritably. He himself had no enthusiasm for the island. . . . The natives were dirty and spat out their betel-juice even on the office step. They were eaten up with scabies and ringworm and fever and were too stupid to have themselves cured. They had innumerable superstitions and tabus, and the higher castes were even worse in that respect than the lower ones. The petty radjas, who after all were no better than bare-footed peasants, squatted about among the litter of their puris and thought themselves the most mighty sovereigns on earth because they could have the heads and hands of their subjects hacked off when they had the mind. But when one of them died, then he was wrapped in white linen and kept in the house till the stink rose to heaven. Boomsmer shuddered at the recollection of this charnel stench and took a quick nip of gin in his turn. The portrait of the Queen, youthful and in full regalia, looked down amiably from the wall.

It is fascinating that the portrait of Queen Wilhelmina plays a prominent ironic role also in the pages of Pramoedya Toer's novel, *This Earth of Mankind*, where the naive Javanese protagonist Minke at first believes that she is a symbol of the shining beauty and optimism for a new age of science and progress which the Dutch will share with the Javanese. By the end of the novel he is sadly disabused of this notion and painfully aware of the tragic discrepancy between the idealism of European philosophy and the brutalities of European colonialism.

Boomsmer's jaundiced views of the Balinese are clearly contrasted by Vicki Baum with her narrator's unabashed love of the exotic life-style of Bali, ranging from religious superstition to sacred dances and from everyday village life in the wet rice fields or sahwahs to the sex life and opium pipes of the feudal lords in their harems. Vicki Baum's *A Tale from Bali* illustrates what cross-cultural literature can do that political, sociological and economic analyses cannot do: it illuminates intuitively a whole culture not by statistical surveys but from within the individual souls of representative Balinese people.

Take this passage, for example, idealizing the Hindu religious rituals of a village temple in rural Bali:

> The two servant girls were laughing happily as they swept the courtyard and fed the pigs. Teragia carefully poured out some of the spring water into a silver vessel, which she then replaced on the tripod in the prayer bale. She fetched spills of sandalwood to burn and lit the sacred fire in a small brazier. She poured more water into a jar, ready for the priest's washings. She brought flowers from many bushes and trees, red for Brahma, blue for Vishnu, white for Shiva. She tied a flower to the silver staff which was used for sprinkling the consecrated water and put the long-handled bell ready in its silken holder. . . . When all was done she surveyed her work with satisfaction. (149)

A Tale from Bali abounds in meticulously observed passages of this kind and often seems like a social geography with an intimate touch. Baum, for example, distinguishes well between the Balinese aristocrats who like Lord Tjokorda Alit are more interested in the aesthetic delights of the gamelan orchestra and the sacred dances that go on all night and those aristocrats who like Gusti Njoman are viewed as traitors because they have chosen to be collaborators with the Dutch and those who are arrogant and unwisely bellicose and wish to drive the Dutch from their sacred island.

The novel has a broad, social landscape and it is only in the depiction of the Chinese that the narrator's customary delicacy and objectivity let her down. She despises the Chinese merchants for their craftiness and their lack of sincerity, saying things like "in any case, lying was part and parcel of his tortuous Chinese mentality." (117) The stranglehold which the Chinese apparently have on trade and the trading fleet is resented by both Dutch and Balinese.

Baum actually ends *A Tale from Bali* with an epilogue in which the Chinese merchant Kwe Tik Tjiang finally receives his 75000 guilders compensation. Tjiang is depicted with the implied loathing of the narrator as a Chinese equivalent of Shakespeare's Shylock demanding his pound of flesh and of course it is his relentless pursuit of profit which has partly caused the Dutch massacre of the Balinese nobility at Badoeng in Southern Bali. The corruption of the old Chinese merchants also figures prominently in Pramoedya Ananta Toer's historical novel, *This Earth of Mankind*, which is set at approximately the same time as Vicki Baum's *A Tale from Bali* at the turn of the century.

A Tale from Bali reveals intimate details of the religious and social and artistic customs of Southern Bali between Sanur and Badoeng by contrasting the life-styles of the lowest caste of wet rice paddy farmers with the luxury of the radja's court. Baum shows the naive rice farmer Pak as he manoeuvres to be able to take a beautiful second wife, Sarnah. But his first wife, the ugly Puglug wants him to marry a second wife who is even uglier than her but who "can carry forty-five coconuts on her head" and who can also "carry three sheaves of rice on a pole like a man and last harvest she threshed more rice than any other woman." (129) Pak wins the beautiful Sarnah only after Sarnah has deliberately mutilated her ear-lobes by tearing out her earrings and thus rendering herself no longer suitable for the elderly radja's harem. By contrast Lord Tjokorda Alit casually marries six new wives, but as he is too bored to attend the ceremony himself, he instead sends his ceremonial sword or kris and the wives swear their oath of marriage to the kris.

Although Vicki Baum clearly loves the Balinese, she does not sentimentalize their life-style. She shows how the artistic brother of Pak has his eyes stabbed out because he flirted with one of the radja's wives in the harem. She depicts the cremation scene in which three widows throw themselves on the funeral pyre of their dead radja. The radja's body is bound inside the funeral lion and as the flames reach their peak and his soul is released to heaven, three of his twenty-four widows prepare to commit ritual suicide:

> The three wives emerged on to the bridge in their white robes. They were giving the last touches to their dresses and their hair, for they wished to look their best when they appeared in heaven. . . . Suddenly the flames shot up as great jars of oil were poured on to them. Two of the wives stepped to the edge of the bridge, exchanged a smiling glance and put their hands to their hair. Pak observed that each held a dove. They both jumped down at the same moment, and as their bodies fell vertically through the air the doves flew away.
>
> "Mbe!" the old man exclaimed with satisfaction, "there go the souls to heaven to find their happiness."
>
> The third wife had meanwhile stepped to the edge of the bridge. She did not smile and her eyes were closed. The fire roared below and she hesitated for the twinkling of an eye. Then she jumped and the dove flew away. "She was afraid," the old man said contemptuously. (414)

A Tale from Bali is ultimately about culture shock and the mutual incomprehension of the Dutch invaders and the Javanese and Balinese peoples. Baum shows the Dutch disguising their lust for power and colonial wealth with sickening hypocrisy and self-righteousness. They exploit the burning of the widows as an excuse for conquering Bali and exploiting its wealth, but the words which they use to justify this bloody conquest are symptomatic of the entire European colonization of the southern hemisphere: "It is our duty to disseminate Dutch ideas and Dutch progress throughout the island. It is our duty to protect the right of the natives and at the same time to root out the cruelties and dark superstitions and customs which cause them so much suffering. You will agree with me gentlemen, when I say that nothing must prevent us from carrying civilization and enlightenment to the colonies which form a part of the great kingdom of the Netherlands." (425)

Of course Multatuli documented in his novel *Max Havelaar,* some seventy years previous to *A Tale from Bali*, the gross discrepancy in Java between civilization and barbaric exploitation. *A Tale from Bali* culminates predictably in the famous military confrontation between the radja's court of Badoeng and the invading Dutch army in 1907. The Dutch army holds its fire and watches in amazement as the radja and his court and his faithful followers emerge at the gateway of the puri temple grounds clad in white and adorned with flowers. They refuse to abandon their cultural pride in their independence and in their way of life. They have dedicated themselves to ceremonial death as a memorial to their religiously based civilization and as a spiritual release to the next world:

> The Balinese were set on death. Nothing in the world could have arrested them in their death-race, neither the howitzers nor the unerring aim of the sharp-shooters, nor the sudden stillness when the firing ceased. Hundreds fell to the enemy's rifles, hundreds more raised their krisses high and plunged them into their breasts, plunging them in above the collar-bone so that the point should reach the heart in the ancient, holy way. . . . The radja's wives had gold crowns on their heads, on which flowers of gold nodded and their hands and arms were loaded with jewels which they tore off and threw to the soldiers with a look of contempt in their large, unconscious eyes. . . . Some of the officers turned their heads aside or put their hands over their eyes. Dekker, for one, was unable to endure the sight of men killing their wives and then themselves, and of mothers driving a kris into their infants' breasts. He turned away and vomited. (502)

Historically this mass suicide by the royal court of Badoeng in Bali is probably the most infamous single incident in the Dutch conquest of the East Indies. Albert Alberts also relates a story of a violent uprising against European, colonial authority. Alberts was a Dutch administrator on the island of Madura near Java and was in Indonesia from 1939 to 1946. His story "The Chase" could be seen as a contrast to Pramoedya Toer's *The Fugitive*, or also to Pramoedya's depiction of the Dutch administration's persecution of his hero Minke in *Awakenings*. Instead of Pramoedya's tragic pathos and the failure of Hardo the fugitive to arouse sufficient Javanese patriotism to rise up against the Japanese army of occupation in 1944—or indeed the failure of Minke to arouse sufficient Javanese patriotism to rise up against the Dutch administration and secret police at the turn of the century—we see a Dutch point of view on the colonies which simply features very unheroic administrators keeping order. This is a startlingly different perspective.

Albert's first-person narrator is half-clown and half a man who likes his comfort, his regular dinners and his afternoon snooze. It is the relentlessness of colonialism's bureaucratic system that forces the narrator as a Dutch provincial administrator to hunt down the unlikely rebel Florines. Florines has apparently burnt down two remote villages in an outburst of rage with any immediately discernible provocation. The narrator doesn't want to kill Florines; in fact he wants to help him escape as he had once helped a panic-stricken, wild boar to escape from hunters into the Indonesian forest. But the narrator's vanity, his need to be seen by his subordinates as a leader, his desire for praise and promotion, all cause him involuntarily to squeeze the trigger and kill the rebel who has run amok. There is no heroism and no deeper meaning. Florines was unarmed.

Indeed this story ends, after the almost farcical cremation of Florines, with the narrator's remorse, a remorse that is signalled only by the symbolism of the dark and the bitter cold on the mountain top after the fire has finally died out.

Contrasted with the passionate rage, the deep patriotism, and the commitment to martyrdom which are evoked by Pramoedya Toer for the thousands of helpless, irrational, rural rebels like Florines throughout Java, Alberts' "The Chase" inevitably seems to be shallow, or at best, the work of embarrassment or guilt.

Joseph Conrad set several of his novels or novellas in and around the Indonesian Archipelago, ranging from *Almayer's Folly* to the short stories, *Lagoon, Youth* and *Karain, A Memory* to one of the last novels that he was to complete, *The Rescue—A Romance of the Shallows* (1920). Conrad begins *The Rescue* with this passage whose words are charged with the electricity of high romanticism:

> The shallow sea that foams and murmurs on the shores of the thousnad islands, big and little, which make up the Malay Archipelago has been for centuries the scene of adventurous undertakings. The vices and the virtues of four nations have been displayed in the conquest of the region even to this day has not been robbed of all the mystery and romance of its past—and the race of men who had fought against the Portuguese, the Spaniards, the Dutch and the English, has not been changed by the unavoidable defeat. They have kept to this day their love of liberty, their fanatical devotion to their chiefs, their blind fidelity in friendships and hate—all their lawful and unlawful instincts. Their country of land and water—for the sea was as much their country as the earth of their island—has fallen a prey to the western race—the reward of superior strength if not of superior virtue.

Conrad may be attracted to the Indonesian Archipelago and to South Asia by the lure of adventure, mystery, romance and exoticism, but he creates profound, moral allegories out of this initial attraction. *The Rescue* is a great novel, but this is not because of the spectacular, armed clash between European adventurers, Illanun pirates, a deposed Rajah and a Koran-quoting Muslim chief called Belarab on the savage coast of Borneo. It is because of the amazing intensity which Conrad injects into the ideals of honour, vision, nobility of spirit, grace, improbable love and the bonds beyond death of a faithful friendship. It is vital to *The Rescue* that these virtues are by no means limited to the Europeans. Conrad is even-handed in his racial distribution of virtue and vice, but it is noticeable and historically understandable that in 1920 he still regards the ultimate conquest of South-East Asia by the technological strength of Europe as inevitable. Conrad finds no particular joy in this prospect and it is interesting that it is the most snobbish, the most stupid and the most despicable character in the novel, Mr. Travers, who says of the Indonesians and the Malays: "And if the inferior race must perish, it is a gain, a step towards the perfecting of society which is the aim of progress." (148)

More than effectively opposed to the insufferable, racist arrogance of this social Darwinism is Mrs. Travers, who wears with pride the gold-threaded costume of a Borneo princess, and who with courage and grace faces her insoluble dilemma of choosing between her love for King Tom Lingard, the visionary adventurer whom she improbably adores, and her duty to her boring husband, Mr. Travers, whom she despises.

Almost inevitably, Conrad focuses for his moral and romantic themes, not on the inhabitants of Borneo, but on the Europeans who are intruders there. The indigenous dwellers in the Indonesian Archipelago play a large role in providing exotic colour and contrasting culture and life-style, but at no stage do we enter a psychological realm where their inner conflicts are revealed to us. This probing into the psyche is reserved for his two main white European characters, King Tom Lingard and Mrs. Travers. They both sacrifice their passion to the dictates of honour with the result that Captain Lingard's vision and spirit are destroyed by despair and grief and Mrs. Travers can look forward to a life of tedium and remorse.

The cause of all this high drama is Captain Lingard's vision of restoring his exiled, aristocratic Wajo friend, Hassim, to his throne as Rajah. It is the improbable faithfulness of this friendship unto death between Hassim and Lingard which is the crux of this novel. The narrator believes that this inter-racial friendship would hardly be understood by most English people, who view the Moors as "wild and inhuman," (405) as "savages" who "treacherously assail(ed)" innocent European visitors (336) and who would view Captain Lingard, not as a man of honour, but as an unprincipled adventurer and a "social impostor." (351) Although Conrad does not penetrate into the inner psyche of his Indonesian/Malayan characters, he does differentiate considerably between their different characters, tribes, appearance and behaviour. Here is his description of Daman, the lord of the pirate chiefs of the Illanuns:

> He advanced alone. The plain hilt of a sword protruded from the open edges of his cloak. The parted edges disclosed also the butts of two flintlock pistols. The Koran in a velvet case hung on his breast by a red cord of silk. He was pious, magnificent, and warlike. (293)
>
> . . . and at his feet two Illanun chiefs, half naked and bedecked with charms and ornaments of bright feathers, of shells, with necklaces of teeth, claws and shining beads, remained cross-legged with their swords across their knees like two bronze idols. Even the plumes of their head-dresses moved not. (292)

Contrast the aesthetic admiration of the narrator in this description with for example first mate Shaw, who is probably a fairly conventional Englishman of his times insofar as he calls the various races of South East Asia all "niggers" (239) who have to be "taught manners and reason" (189) "by their betters—missionaries, and such like au-thorities." (22) Shaw is outraged that "niggers" should be permitted by the Captain into the sacred "cuddy" or captain's cabin.

It is interesting to contrast for example Pramoedya Ananta Toer's moral outrage in *Awakenings* that Dutchmen should have been permitted by law to buy Indonesian girls as mistresses or concubines with Joseph Conrad's impassive or even almost humorous noting that the adventurer Joergenson, who has settled pemanently in the East Indies, has bought his life companion with "three hundred dollars and several brass guns." (105) Nevertheless, one should also note that Joergensen is faithful unto death to his mistress and ensures that she will be provided for in the event of his death. Conrad also has his narrator relate a side-story about a Bali girl who threw a red blossom at a good-looking Frenchman and who, because she was the property of the Rajah's nephew, was condemned to death and executed. This story of innocent but catastrophic inter-racial flirtation culminates in this highly ironic dialogue between the racist Shaw and culturally open Captain Lingard:

> "Would those savages kill a woman for that?" asked Shaw, incredulously.
>
> "Aye! They are pretty moral there." (21)

Historically and geographically, *The Rescue* is located on the rebellious fringe of the Dutch East Indies empire. It is some years, according to the narrator, since "Sir Thomas Cochrane swept along the Borneo coast" and "did a rare lot of fighting," (23) but this doesn't change the fact that the coast and the jungle are still full of untamed chieftains and bands of pirates. The chief of the Shore of Refuge, Belarab, is himself a refugee from his family's armed conflicts with the Dutch in Sumatra. Lone European adventurers like Captain Lingard and old Captain Joergenson, who have chosen to stay permanently in the Indonesian Archipelago and make it their home, take considerable pleasure in siding with their Mohammedans against the Dutch, (103) partly out of a desire to frustrate the Dutch and partly out of genuine friendship and empathy with the inhabitants of the Archipelago. But their commitment to their inter-racial friendships is no more passionate than their love for the ships and neither is destined to bring them harmony or prosperity or peace of soul.

It is barely a decade that separates Joseph Conrad's *The Rescue* from Madelon Lulofs' *Rubber* and yet their depictions of the Dutch East Indies are worlds apart. The exotic adventurers, the piracy and the revolutions of Rajahs are completely lost from sight. Instead Lulofs portrays the back-breaking work and the heavy monotony of the rubber plantations of East Sumatra. This is a world of order, discipline, commercial exploitation of the Javanese coolies and white plantation managers and their assistants out to amass big capital on which they can base their retirement in luxury back home in Holland.

Rubber captures the period of the great rubber boom in the 1920s and ends when the bottom drops out of the rubber market in the late 1920s and mad speculation in tobacco and oil on the stock market finishes with the Wall Street crash and the depression of the 1930s. Lulofs does not so much give a portrait of Sumatra and the peoples of the East Indies as a portrait of the planters and their ambivalent attitude towards the Dutch colony. The focus is very much on the white planters' life-style. Nevertheless, there is in the background some very revealing pictures of the coolies and their life-style.

Lulofs' portrait of the climate and landscape and life-style of the planters in East Sumatra is anything but joyful. She speaks of the "torpor of the tropics" and expresses her distaste for the coastal mud swamps and the "opaque green forest." But the rubber plantations are even more negatively portrayed:

> Then, abruptly, the road came out into the new plantation, Tumbuk Tinggih. Here the mighty forest had been cut away, burnt, annihilated. Between two rows of low hills lay the flat strip of dull brown land, colourless, featureless, endless. . . . And over all this endless solitude, this mournful monotony, glowed the hot shimmering sky, the blinding sunlight. . . . On this sad, inhospitable, repulsive land the coolies were setting out sticks to mark the places where the young rubber trees were to be planted.

This tropical landscape is contrasted nostalgically with the fresh Spring weather of Holland and the cool winds on the sand-dunes, the shops and the civilization of the Dutch cities. All the plantation managers yearn for their furlough of five months every five years in Holland, and yet when they return to Holland, they find that they have become estranged from it. They have become second class citizens, colonials. Their manners have become too free and easy; they no longer fit into the tight-lipped bourgeois discipline of their native country. They have become exiles without a home.

Their only comfort is the fortune which they have amassed in the East Indies from their huge salaries and their enormous salary bonuses during the rubber boom. They return to Holland after five to twenty years with capital ranging from 60,000 guilders, which is really not enough, to three hundred thousand guilders. But to their amazement, they find that they now miss their work on the rubber plantations. They have nothing to do. They sink into alcoholicism in Holland and keep company with gold-digging prostitutes. In any case, by the time they are in their forties, their bodies are ravaged by tropical diseases such as malaria and dysentery and their "nerves are rotten," destroyed by the never-ending heat and the monotony of the rubber plantations and the alcoholic orgies of their private clubs in East Sumatra.

Lulofs is, however, a sharp observer. She is able to give striking descriptions of the Malay or Chinese or Japanese women who become the housekeepers and the long-term mistresses of these planters. Here is her memorable description of the teeming street life just outside the Dutch private club:

> Rickshaws and carriages rolled by noiselessly, Chinese coolies ran past, naked to the waist and sweating. . . . Bataks, Malays and Chinese offered goods for sale—batik stuff, and gold and silver embroideries, copper and silver, porcelain, weapons. Blink beggars stood with outstretched hands in front to the terrace until the servants chased them away. British Indians passed by, tall and lean, wearing nothing but a cloth round their loins. . . . On their heads were turbans. Most of them were drunk. There were native women of Deli, tall, slender, majestic. . . . In their nostrils were little studs of gold. They walked like queens; they turned their delicately cut, dark, mobile faces towards every little incident of the street.
>
> They were in striking contrast to the Malay women—small, graceful, dressed in rustling sarongs and silken vests, their heads wrapped in a veil, their bare feet covered by small slippers of gold-stitched velvet. There were Chinese women too, masculine looking in trousers and tight vests, their hair straight and arranged in one smooth swathe, their feet in wooden slippers. The Japanese women, tiny and decorative in their kimonos with the long hanging sleeves and their complicated hair dressing of three buns and one swathe, were like porcelain dolls.
>
> The Sikhs, their sculptured heads under immense turbans, walked past majestically. British Indian money-lenders—fat, well-fed, with dark-oily skins, their heads shaven and wrapped in snow-white cloths—slipped through the throng. (45-46)

Small wonder that many of the Dutch planters were happy enough to make do with housekeeper-mistresses from among this exotic melange, rather than bring out flighty and often spoilt Dutch wives, who hated and resented their husbands' isolated postings and compensate, according to Lulofs, with increasingly luxurious and licentious champagne and rum parties at their private planters' clubs. Supporting this enormous Dutch wealth is the sweated labour of the imported Javanese contract coolies. Lulofs comments: "Once a person contracted, he lost all his rights and his humanity. Signing the contract meant that one had to live by the clock, always do what one was ordered, take quinine and castor oil." (80)

Every day from half-past five in the morning till half-past in the afternoon, "the half-naked, sweating, toiling coolies" clear the jungle and plant the rubber trees. Cynically the plantation managers encourage the coolies to the gambling shed where they spend the whole night gambling away their wages. (213) That way they cannot return home to Java after their contract has finished. Instead they have to stay for another term of sweated labour in the jungles of East Sumatra.

Small wonder that some of the Hadjis, the men who had made the sacred pilgrimage to Mecca, urge the coolies on to agitate "against everything European" (186) and small wonder that every so often a coolie runs amok and murders a Dutch supervisor with his knife. The Dutchman is buried with full ceremony; the coolie is duly tried and found guilty and eventually executed; and everyone returns to the labour in the rubber plantations whose excesses and racist exploitation are at the basis of the crime.

Lulofs implies that many of the Dutch workers were decent enough as individuals, but there is little explicit insistence in her novel—as there had been seventy years previously in Multatuli's *Max Havelaar*—that this systematic, pseudo-slavery of the Javanese peasants by the Dutch should be immediately stopped. Lulofs concentrates her focus far rather on the question of whether the Dutch planters and their Dutch wives werre gaining life-fulfilment in their tortured self-exile from their beloved Holland.

Post-war Australian fiction writers on Indonesia, like Jon Cleary in *The Long Pursuit*, Christopher Koch in *The Year of Living Dangerously*, Blanche d'Alpuget in *Monkeys in the Dark* and Gerard Lee in *Troppo Man*—and one could of course also draw parallels with Blanch d'-Alpuget on Malaysia in *Turtle Beach* and Robert Drewe on the Philippines in *A Cry in the Jungle Bar*—tend to focus more on a basically sympathetic but also very critical and even horrified assessment of political and economic mismanagement, racism, religious superstition, mass poverty, corruption and ideological strife in postcolonial South East Asia.

Jon Cleary's *The Long Pursuit* is really a slick war-thriller and its focus on non-stop guerilla action and its cliches about national identity at first glance hardly seem to offer an appropriate basis for an insightful assessment of Indonesian society. Nevertheless, the novel does record some of the paradoxes of European-South East Asian relations at a crucial turning-point in time, namely the early days of the Japanese occupation of Sumatra.

Cleary is able to use the advantages of wisdom in hindsight to show how the Javanese and the Sumatrans were hoodwinked in the early 1940s by the Japanese posing as fellow-Asians and as liberators from the imperialist Dutch and British. The Javanese and Sumatrans at first believed the Japanese propaganda about an "Asian Joint-Prosperity Sphere" and Cleary shows how they cooperated in imprisoning the Dutch administrators and engineers and running the archipelago's industrial and commercial facilities to assist the Japanese war-effort.

The PNI or Communist leader from Java, Kamar, and his friend Ahmat will not allow the motley group of British/ American/ Dutch/ Australian amateur-saboteurs to blow up the Palembang oil refinery in Sumatra because, as Ahmat says: "The refineries belong to us now. The Japanese have told us they want us to help them run Sumatra—the Hollanders will never be back."

The Dutch girl Elizabeth, whose great-grandfather married a Sumatran princess, cannot understand the murderous hatred of the Sumatrans as they throw off the imperialist Dutch yoke. She remembers her father's much applauded speech just before the war in defence of empire: "If we Hollanders moved out, someone else would only move in. Politics like nature abhors a vacuum. The Indonesians should realize that we are here as much for their good as for our own. This is our land as much as theirs. Three centuries gives us more than a leasehold, it gives us freehold right." (199)

This is much the same apologia as the Afrikanners have used in South Africa. Ethically it is an invalid argument because as an attempt at the justification of colonial exploitation and enslavement of indigenous peoples, it can only argue that all those who hold technological power are as greedy and as ruthless as they are. If they do not continue to commit the evil of colonial dictatorship, some other nation will do it instead. Of course it must also be conceded that the brief history of the postcolonialist era in Africa and Asia indicates that greedy and ruthless dictators can also be of the same race as the oppressed, indigenous people. Liberation of countries in South East Asia, Africa and South America has not often resulted in democratic liberation of the individual or a fair sharing of natural resources among the indigenous people. This generalization applies reasonably well to the post-war, political and economic organization of Indonesia under both Sukarno and Suharto. Nevertheless, the failings of postcolonial governments are hardly an ethical justification of European colonialism in the southern hemisphere in the preceding three centuries.

Kamar express some of the bitterness of Indonesians against the Dutch when he points out a Dutch school in Sumatra that is "for Dutch children only." (187) As Kamar says: "A little knowledge is a dangerous thing. So is too much education. It breeds revolution. So the Dutch never gave us too much education. They were like the British, captain. No offence." (187)

Parmoedya Toer in *Awakenings* and in his stories about his father's work as a poorly paid teacher of his fellow-Javanese shows his intense awareness of the political uses of education in progressing towards nationalist revolution.

There is of course a quite different side to colonialism. This is the side in which the colonial overlords come to feel admiration for the courage of the conquered people and awe for their religious culture, which in their own lands has often been displaced by a worship of technology and materialism. Elizabeth recalls the legendary courage of the Prince of Badoeng and the 250 men, women and children of his royal family who dressed in their most magnificent clothes and jewellery as they participated in a *puputan* and challenged the Dutch invaders to murder them.

In Jon Cleary's *The Long Pursuit*, the European refugees stumble on the imposing stupas and Bodhisattvas of Belan Koup in the Sumatran jungle where a band of Dutch guerillas have been slaughtered by PNI fighters. The English military captain Maynard looks at the magnificent ruins of Belan Koup and is inspired to feel the significant lack of religiosity in his own Western life-style:

> The Englishman looked up and for the first time saw the status of the Buddha, seated on a stone lotus, gazing down at him with unseeing eyes, lost in a state of tranquillity that the pale green stone suggested more than living flesh ever could have. A complacently habitual Anglican, going to church as a matter of social form, he knew suddenly that the eyes of the stone saints in the cathedrals of England had never looked into his soul as did these green eyes staring down at him now. He was not converted to another religion, but suddenly made aware of his shabby, careless approach to his own. (160)

This reaction to Eastern religiosity is a very important and recurring image in Western responses to South East Asian cultures. There is an epiphany of a vital lack in Western materialism, a lack of spirituality.

Awareness of Indonesia has apparently even penetrated into popular Australian fiction. The bibliography of *Asia in Western Fiction* lists a detective novel by Arthur Upfield, which features a half-Aboriginal sleuth called Napoleon Bonaparte, as being about Indonesia. This is of course nonsense; it is about Aborigines in the remote Kimberley region of Western Australia. Nevertheless, in the denouement it is revealed that Indonesian spies had illegally entered Australia in order to promise the Aborigines liberation from white Australians and access to some kind of white man's cargo cult of unlimited tucker and tobacco. I hesitate to calculate in how many different ways this hypothesis is racist! But worse is to come. As Napoleon Bonaparte says of the Indonesians: "These Asians are confident they will eventually gain Dutch New Guinea through the Western Nations' passion for compromise or appeasement, which of course is always accepted as weakness, and that, having gained this territory, they will proceed to work for the other half of the Island, governed by Australia. Following success there, they will demand, with grounds for hope, that the northern half of Australia should be surrendered to them." (*The Will of the Tribe* 234)

It is fascinating to reflect that in the space of a mere thirty years, from Madelon Lulofs' *Rubber* in 1930s to Arthur Upfield's *The Will of the Tribe* in the 1960s, the image of Indonesia in western fiction has gone from sweated coolie labour in a colonial Dutch empire to an independent nation bent on expanding its island empire in a big way at the expense of Australia.

The images of Malaysia, Indonesia and the Philippines projected by our mass media with TV mini-series such as *Embassy*, or front page corruption allegations about Madam Suharto and Imelda Marcos, or morally justifiable condemnations of the Indonesian massacre of civilians in East Timor, or historically inaccurate and sensationalist film scenes such as the mythical slaughter of Hoa Chinese boat people on the beaches of Malaysia in Blanche d'Alpuget's *Turtle Beach* have brought Australia into repeated conflict with the governments of South East Asia which do not permit such inefficient luxuries as an independent press or a politically insensitive film industry, to say nothing of muck-raking.

Blanche d'Alpuget's *Monkeys in the Dark* gives some racy, gossippy impressions of the diplomatic high life in Jakarta one year after the abortive Communist uprising and the reactionary coup of General Suharto in 1965. The novels hinge on the attempts of Pro-Sukarno, left-wing forces to mount a counter-revolution against the New Order of the military elite. The novel reaches its political climax with President Sukarno's last mass rally and Independence Day commemoration speech. In this speech Sukarno, who is already a quasi-prisoner of General Suharto, delivers his last attack on capitalist imperialism, neo-colonialism, the American invasion of Vietnam and the policies of the Indonesian New Order. He is called "the old magician . . . unrepentant, and dancing in the air." He harangues the crowd: "'Oh my people, if you abandon our history you will face a vacuum. You will stand on emptiness, confused. Your continuing struggle will become meaningless and undirected. Life for you will be no more than running amok. Running amok—like monkeys trapped in the dark!'" (122)

There is a lot of running amok in *Monkeys in the Dark*, but thanks to d'Alpuget's satiric pen, it is much more the Westen diplomats who behave "like monkeys trapped in the dark." Their partying, gossiping, boozing, bi-sexual, screaming queen hi-jinx and espionage would I am sure produce exhaustion and primitive aging in normal human beings who were not fuelled up with d'Alpuget's kickapoo juice.

The Indonesian characters featured in *Monkeys in the Dark* include the poet and pro-Sukarno counter-revolutionary Maruli who sexually exploits the Australian Embassy's publicity officer Alex. Also featured is the corrupt, scheming powerful Sutrisno who was allegedly castrated during the revolution and who now hobnobs with Japanese pulp millers, imprisons the revolutionary Maruli and is himself very nearly assassinated in Singapore. Then there is the traitor Usman who sells secrets about the pro-Sukarno underground to Australian spies and who is killed by a Jakarta military policeman who mistakenly thinks he is a bantji male-prostitute evading arrest. Usman bleeds to death in the foyer of a Jakarta hospital because the hospital has no blood for transfusion.

Monkeys in the Dark presents the upper classes of Jakarta as devoted to the struggle for power and to the trapping and prestige of power and therefore obsessed with the extermination of all egalitarian communists. As Mrs Ibu Sularto says:

> "The communists murdered our six hero generals and threw their bodies in the Crocodile Hole." Dropping her voice still lower, so that only Alex could hear, she murmured, "The communists cut off their . . ." vaguely indicating her lap ". . . and pulled out their eyes. Thanks be to God that their coup failed! And that the people rose to crush them! The people swore to kill one hundred thousand communists for every murdered hero. . . . In six more weeks it will be a year since the murders at the Crocodile Hole, since General Nasution's little daughter was shot dead." (110)

D'Alpuget inevitably makes lively gossip about Indonesian corruption. The character Claude at a party points to a woman, saying: "She's wife of the Old Order governor of the State Bank, who's going on trial next month. He embezzled virtually all the country's foreign exchange and spent it on his wives. He's rumoured to have twenty-eight of them, which must be rather expensive when they all like diamonds and baby Mercedes and shopping in Rome. Nice earrings she's wearing." (144)

Corruption allegedly is way of life. Chinese Dr Tan is philosophical "when Indonesian customs officials confiscated his shipments of penicillin and insulin and sold them at high prices to the public hospital." (149)

Jakarta of these years is nervous and tense, subject to nightly curfews, scattered gunfire, student street demonstrations against Sukarno, military street blockades, check-ups on identity passes, illegal printing of subversive propaganda pamphlets, and stockpiling of weapons. Racial tension and culture clash abound, even in diplomatic circles. Australians call the Indonesians "nig-nogs" and the waiters at the Ramayana Bar are called "Piss Monkey" to their faces. (19) This personal tension occurs in the framework of a foreign policy clash in which various scenarios are allegedly considered by Australian espionage: "the possibility of a hostile Indonesia blockading Australian shipping and air routes; the lunatic Right in Australian politics becoming hysterical and forcing excessive defence spending when Indonesia appeared aggressive; the trade relationship, particularly oil; New Guinea border problems; the military threat to New Guinea and the panic that would cause in Australia." (105)

On the other hand the Indonesians joke about the dilapidated condition of the roads on which a mythical Indonesian invasion army would have to march south from Jakarta. D'Alpuget inevitably includes in her images of Indonesia the horrific living conditions of the urban poor. The labour of the betjak-drivers and the coolies with their hand-carts appeals the novel's female protagonist Alex. As Alex is driven home for lunch, she notices: "how rotten the city was smelling: the sweet clove smoke could no longer mask the stench of the canals in which water had now ceased to flow. The canals had turned into witches' brews, in which faces floated, but the city's poor had nowhere else to wash or defecate." (133) Also, as David says to Alex:

> It's the end of the dry season, dearie. Gets on everybody's nerves. Starving mosquitoes and stinkin' canals. And the cholera. It starts around now in those kampongs near Tjiliwung; then the wet season comes and it gets worse. . . . Nothing in the newspapers, of

> course, until there's no room left in the hospitals. Then there's a little paragraph saying, "Five hundred cases of cholera have been confirmed in the Greater Jakarta area, the Director-General of Health said on Thursday." (132)

But the dominant focus of the culture clash between Australia and Indonesia is on politics, and specifically on the brutality and militarization of Indonesian politics. So, we hear of a man who is punished by having his right arm and his left leg amputated and about another man who is castrated as a punishment. Then there is the businessman Sutrisno who calls an acquaintance "Brother" knowing that tomorrow he will be arrested and then executed.

The difference between Indonesia and Australia is grotesquely illustrated by an incident involving a character called Mother Plastic in the slums of Jakarta. Mother Plastic wears only a see-through plastic raincoat. As a genuine eccentric she refuses to concede that she is naked and joins in the street social life in a vigorous way. No action is taken against her by the Indonesian police. This prompts Alex to observe that in Australia: "We lock up mad people. They gaol intellectuals." (138) This is a shrewd observation about different kinds of conformism and the relevance of the intellectual to the community in two very different countries.

Timothy Mo takes up the theme of Indonesia's militarism and its foreign policy relationship with Australia in his brilliantly narrated work, *The Redundancy of Courage* (1991). *The Redundancy of Courage* is a sophisticated account of the "malais'" brutal invasion of an island called Danu which is less than one hour by air from the Northern Territory. (17) The former ruling inhabitants of Danu before the nationalist-communist uprising had Portuguese names like Arsenio Remedio and Sonia Ferreira. The invading cherry and purple beret malais use "Soviet-pattern assault rifles which their deposed President has bequeathed them." (19) The Chinese shopkeepers of Danu are rounded up and murdered with cold deliberation and so too is the last Australian journalist on the island, Bill Mabbeley. Their bodies are kicked off the edge of the jetty into the sea where they drift the jelly blubbers in the tide. These are of course all images of Indonesian militarism and brutality in the 1975 invasion of East Timor. They are meant to have, and do have, a shocking impact on Western and especially Australian readers.

The Redundancy of Courage presents an unflattering image of a greedy and ruthless Indonesian military. This perspective is perhaps understandable insofar as the first-person narrator is a Chinese citizen of

East Timor and his report shows how the Indonesian army reduced the East Timorese population from 750,000 to under 500,000. It might be thought that Timothy Mo's novel, insofar as the Indonesians are aware of its existence, could do as much damage to Australian-Indonesian commercial relations as Blanche d'Alpuget's *Turtle Beach* did to Australian-Malaysian relations. But then *Turtle Beach* was relatively unknown as a novel and it only caused a sensation when it was filmed and the media suddenly realized that the Malaysian slaughter on the beach of Hoa Chinese boat people was an historically unfounded slander of the Malaysians' human rights record.

By contrast *The Redundancy of Courage* seems to be meticulously researched down to the brand of rifles, bullets and aeroplanes used by the Indonesian invaders and the guerillas' life-style and military strategies in the inaccessible highlands. Becuase the Chinese narrator is a self-confessed, unthreatening "pansy" and because he is ingenious and wily, he wins the confidence not only of the East Timorese guerillas (who are allegedly still making "shrunken heads" of their victims, cf. 231) but also of an Indonesian army colonel and his wife and child. This results in some intimate, insightful and not entirely unsympathetic portrayals of the colonel's wife. She courts prestige for her husband and for herself and to achieve this end she will exploit any means available to her including humbly seeking the advice of her Chinese "pansy"-servant and deceiving and insidiously threatening visiting international journalists. The Chinese narrator makes a point of stressing the corruption, thievery and bribery of Indonesian officials:

> I'd say the *malai* military were the lineal descendants of the piratical rajahs and sultans in their island nests. You trod carefully. Their moods were arbitrary. . . . The *malais* were great thieves. They were one of the corruptest nations in Asia. Believe me, that is to say something. They stole everything in Danu, including what was nailed down. Refrigerators, cars, air-conditioners, all got loaded up in front of the amazed eyes of the Danuese and shipped back to the *malai* capital. These were the perquisites of senior officers. (103-4)

Not that the Chinese narrator, Adolph Ng, is any more flattering about the Chinese business people of South East Asia. As he himself says: "It was a sore point for the Danuese that the Chinese would suck them dry, then send the money off the island in the shape of remittances to Taiwan, China, Macao, and Hong Kong." (89)

In the end the Chinese narrator achieves liberation from his quasi-slavery as a servant with the Indonesian colonel by bribing him with dollars from an American bank account, while maintaining the exquisite pretence that together the two of them are really bribing a difficult third person high up in the bureaucracy. The pre-requisite for the success of this bribery is that Adolph Ng has saved the life of the son of the colonel and his wife. As Adolph says of the wife:

> She had a conscience—or rather she had what was an Asian's limited version of a social morality, the strong sense of a favour done and an obligation to requite. She couldn't pass over that. The bad side of it was all the things which afflicted the malais: nepotism, corruption; the good side of it was the desire not to show ingratitude. 'Do unto others as you would be done by' was a more positive social prescription of societies like Toronto but 'Scratch my back and I'll scratch yours' was a workable Asian alternative. (394)

The biggest surprise in *The Redundancy of Courage* is saved up for the end. The narrator alleges that the Indonesian invasion of East Timor wasn't just an act of land-grabbing. It was primarily motivated by the American navy's need of the deep-water channel off East Timor for its nuclear submarines. The American President was allegedly in Jakarta the day before the Indonesian invasion of East Timor and the Americans provided military assistance and aeroplanes in order to prevent this deep-water sea-channel remaining in East Timorese Communist (FAKOUM) control. (405)

Not only is the USA implicated in such callous international piracy and genocide of the East Timorese; so too is Australia. The vital radio link to the world of the East Timorese independence fighters, their only way of telling the world the truth, is through Australia. Adolph has this to say about that radio link: "The best hut in the camp, the thickest thatched, the driest—waterproof even after two and a half months of downpour—and the most closely guarded, was not Osvaldo's. It was the radio hut. This was their line to the world, via the Australian Northern Territory distress network, meant for the Flying Doctor. They could get word to the world through this—until the Aussie government did the *malais* a favour and cut the line." (140)

The Redundancy of Courage combines the virtues of an international military thriller—showing first hand, authentic details of the mysterious guerillas and the Indonesian army—with a framework of international, political expediency, power-lust and cynicism. The rich nations get richer and the poor colonized minorities get poorer and only the wily

Chinese middleman survives to make another dollar or another escudos in another continent.

In *Troppo Man* Gerard Lee dramatizes the commercialization of Balinese religious life-style and art through tourism. In passing he satirizes the hordes of vulgar Australian tourists who seem to wish to export Bondi Beach to Kuta Beach for their holidays—seeking sex and surf, beer and beach as the summit of simple hedonism. In Kuta everyone is selling something, including the "personal taximan" of a "pery expensip limousine" who says "I hap Trance Dance, Puppet Show, Pub Crawl" or "a woman."

Bali is seen in *Troppo Man* through the outraged eyes of prissy, pedantic Matthew, a wimp of an ex-school teacher who preaches sermons to total strangers about the tourism rape of Balinese culture and who reserves a virulent hatred for what he sees as American cultural imperialism.

By contrast, the lovable and relaxingly sociable Dewi, the owner of the losman in Ubud where most of the cross-cultural mingling takes place, reveals in four short sentences some of the grotesque truth hidden behind the tourism-facade of Bali and Ubud: "My husband dead. Dey kill him in '65. Dey tell everyone he is communist but not true. Try to help piple only." (41)

Matthew trying altogether too hard to show respect for Balinese artistic traditions, constantly commits cultural bloopers. He loses his money to a fast-talking, artist-swindler and womanizer called Nyoman. Nyoman misuses some of this money to throw an old man out of his subsistence-refuge onto the street.

Again by contrast with Matthew, young Pete, who is unashamedly Australian with "Fosters, . . . Mambo t-shirts . . . custom-made surf boards" (182) and Sydney slang, is instinctively loved by the Balinese in Ubud because he is natural and authentic and genuinely friendly, even when he puts his foot in it culturally.

Matthew is diagnosed by an American professor of anthropology in Ubud as having "Noble Savage Syndrome": "a lot of people get it the first time they come to Bali. They think the Balinese are living in perfect harmony and can't do anything wrong. They treat the whole island like it's a cathedral. The Church of the Noble Savage, Burditt called it." (96)

Unfortunately Gerard Lee's further exploration of Balinese paradoxes gets overwhelmed by impish Matthew's sexual problems. A far more substantial and profound account of Australian-Indonesian culture-clash is to be found in Christopher Koch's *The Year of Living Dangerously*.

Christopher Koch realizes that we Australians will need a new ethos and a new national mythology to cope with our radical turnabout from being and English colony until 1901 and a European-oriented nation until the 1950s. In today's work our trade, our immigration and our active participation in Asian/Pacific politics and wars are making us more and more a part of South East Asia. *The Year of Living Dangerouly* attempts to provide this new mythology as an idealistic quest for a kind of cross-cultural Holy Grail. (19)

Unlike *Troppo Man*, the thrust of *The Year of Living Dangerously* is not just cross-culturally erotic, it is also political and religious. The main character is undoubtedly the Chinese-Australian dwarf, Billy Kwan. Billy sees his life as a philosophical crusade of great intensity and urgency. He must find the answer to the questions posed in the Gospels (Luke 3, 10) and echoed by the aged seeker Tolstoy: "What then must we do?" That is, what is morally required of us affluent Westerners when we are confronted with the poverty, disease and misery of the third world in general and Indonesia in particular?

Billy Kwan lives in two kinds of personal hell. His first hell is sexual: he has the sexual needs of a normal man but cannot hope to fulfil these needs because of his dwarfishness. His second hell is that he is a hybrid who cannot find an environment to which he belongs, which he can declare to be his home. He is hybrid because he is half Chinese and half Australian, but is accepted by no racial group. He is also hybrid because he is not a complete dwarf: he is on the frustrating verge of the lowest height considered to be within the bounds of normalcy. But he shares the hybrid existence of famous dwarfs through the ages of history insofar as he plays the clown and the fool in public but carries out secret studies in a private quest for wisdom.

Billy tries to emerge from his hell through intense idealism. He is idealistic in his search for perfect friendship with cynical Australian journalists Guy Hamilton and he is equally uncompromising in his naive and misplaced hero-worship of President Sukarno. The heaven that Billy seeks is both personally and politically utopian. No mere mortal, whether a president or mere journalist, can hope to live up to Billy's idealistic expectations. Billy's resultant disillusion drops him into the bottomless pit of despair. He is a worse hell than when he began his quest. It is partly from Billy's almost insane desperation that *The Year of Living Dangerously* is driven on to conflict and catastrophe.

Sukarno is also perceived to be as hybrid and as flawed as Billy. He is ironically depicted as the God Vishnu swooping down from the clouds in his white helicopter (12) but he is also squalidly subject to sexual promiscuity. This promiscuity is not seen as joyful but is interpreted by the Great Wally in *The Year of Living Dangerously* as "Sarinahism."

(217) Sarinah was the family servant with whom Sukarno shared his bed when he was a little boy. Sukarno named the big new department store after his beloved Sarinah and perhaps his promiscuity in adulthood was only a search to replace her.

The minor characters in *The Year of Living Dangerously* are all woven into this complex web of sexual and political chaos. It is not only President Sukarno who is living dangerously in this last year of his real reign, 1965. All of the other characters in the novel are also living dangerously. They are all shown to suffer frustration and failure. In the sexual sphere, for example, there is the Great Wally who is increasingly tormented by his lust for the bantjis, the ululating boy-girl prostitutes of Jakarta. When his secret is betrayed to the Indonesian authorities, they use it as an excuse to deport him and thus get rid of his embarrassingly well-informed political reports to the Western world.

The New Zealand reporter Kevin Condon tries to relieve himself of his sexual frustration by driving his battered little Fiat around taking furtive photographs of poor Indonesian peasant women exposing their breasts while they wash themselves in the sewerage canals. As the narrator puts it: "he is romantically in love with his own perpetual frustration." The Canadian reporter Curtis drives out to the prostitutes at the Jakarta cemetery who expose themselves in his headlights in order to prove that they are not banshee boy-girls but the real thing. Curtis has reduced the mystery of love to the tormented circle of hell: lust and clap, lust and clap.

The Indonesian counterpart of Colonel Henderson is the minor Communist Party leader Kumar. Kumar is obliged to conceal his political commitment in order to retain his lucrative and informative job as Guy Hamilton's assistant. His real authority is revealed only when he stops the PKI mob from kiling Billy and Guy in the streets of Jakarta and at the end of the novel when he reveals that he speaks fluent Russian (as well as English), having been a student in Leningrad. Kumar is a failure politically because his Communist Party fifth column is defeated on the brink of the big breakthrough by General Suharto's armed forces. Kumar dreams as fervently as does billy Kwan of a just society in which wealth is distributed according to need and not corruptly hoarded by the greedy few. In the end he is obliged to admit sadly that this is only an unattainable dream, or as he puts it in the most poignant phrase in the novel: "it is water from the moon." Kumar will be hunted to his probable death just as up to half a million communists and Chinese were hunted to their death throughout Indonesia in the bloodbath that followed the murder of the six Indonesian army generals in 1965. But in the novel Kumar does not rely on Guy for escape at all. On the contrary, he retains a fiercely independent posture at the end saying: "Mr. Billy Kwan was right. . . . Westerners have not many answers any more. . . . We will win because we know what we believe—and you believe in nothing but your pleasures." (289-90)

Major and minor characters in the *The Year of Living Dangerously* are therefore integrated in the novel's themes of failure of frustration of the dream of honest friendship in a just society. Billy Kwan explains his failure mythologically when he quotes from the *Bhagavad Gita* a line spoken by the God Krishna as advice to the Prince Arjuna: "Greedy lust and anger: this is the enemy of the soul. All is clouded by desire, Arjuna: as fire by smoke, as a mirror by dust." (82) Billy attempts to overcome these confusing clouds of desire by deliberately refraining from sex and by devoting himself to his vision of the ideal friendship and the ideal society. He gives financial support to the Jakarta slum-family of Ibu and her two children and refuses her puzzled offer of sex in order to repay his generosity. Billy is trying to practice the Christian golden rule of giving love as a response to the fomenting question of Luke 3, 10 "What then must we do?" The implication is that if we all go forth and do likewise, then we do not need to worry about the insoluble political problems of society because they will solve themselves. But Billy is defeated here, too, by ignorance and disease. Ibu and her family bathe in the open sewerage canals of Jakarta and her infant son dies of gastroenteritis. Ibu is taken away presumably to earn her meagre living by prostitution. Billy has lost the family that he could never have by normal means and his Christian experiment has failed.

As a tragic hero Billy knows no compromise: he insists on the ideal or nothing. Exiled from the Wayang journalists' club because he is thought (wrongly) to have betrayed the Great Wally to the Indonesian authorities, he catches in isolation his insane suicidal scheme to confront Sukarno at a public rally with a daubed sheet hanging from a hotel window: "Sukarno feed you people!" Billy is murdered by the dictator's security police and becomes an unknown martyr to the cause of the just society. But it is Billy's death that inspires Guy Hamilton to a change of heart about the meaning of friendship, love and commitment and in this sense Billy's death has not been in vain.

Reverence for religious myth provides the basis of Billy Kwan's opposition to the materialistic ideology of Marxism. Under Comrade Aidit's Marxism, claims Billy in his passionate, unread appeal: "The myths would be perverted into propaganda, the life of the spirit stilled in the name of the full belly, and love of God made an offence. Islam would be extinguished, and so would joy. . . . Unless we love god and reverence life, we are bound for extinction."

Colonial and Canonical Control over Third World Writers

SEODIAL DEENA

(a) Overview of the socio-economic and political complications

The task of global representation falls into the hands of Third World writers after years of misrepresentation by the colonizers. According to Walter Rodney, the colonies could not rely on the writers from the European empires to represent a true picture about the events of colonization. Commenting on the paradox of underdevelopment,[1] Rodney illustrates how one bourgeois economist fails to provide "a historical explanation" or "a relationship of exploitation," but advances "a biblical explanation" by quoting Matthew 25:29 "For unto everyone that hath shall be given, and he shall have abundance; but from him that hath not shall be taken away even that which he hath." (20-21) The bourgeois economist boldly concludes that "the story of the 'hath nots' is the story of the modern underdeveloped countries."[2]

Dan Izevbaye provides an African perspective of this point in "The Igbo as Exceptional Colonial Subjects: Fictionalizing an Abnormal Historical Situation," by pointing out the damaging effects of such a biased representation of colonization: "The colonial perception of Africans and their civilization, as reflected in European literature and ethnography, so affected the social and psychological state of Africa that [writers like] Achebe must retell the story of the African past to educate Europeans and Africans alike." (45) This process of decolonization or retelling of the story embarked upon by many Third World writers such as Chinua Achebe, Ngugi wa Thiong'o, Wole Soyinka, Camara Laye, Mongo Beti, Ferdinand Oyono, Buchi Emecheta, Gabriel Okara, Sembene Ousmane, Elechi Amadi, Alex La Guma, Bessie Head (Africa); Mulk Raj Anand, R.K. Narayan, Raja Rao, Salman Rushdie, Kamala Markandaya, Farrukh Dhondy, Jussawalla (India); George Lamming, V.S. Naipaul, Wilson Harris, Samuel Selvon, Louise Bennett, Jan Carew, John Hearne, Jamaica Kincaid, and Derek Walcott (Caribbean),[3] is a challenging one since it involves shattering the status quo. To shatter the status quo, these writers have to create what Said has called "an opposing point of view, perspective, consciousness" to counter act "the unitary web of vision" entrenched in the dominant criticism."[4]

Most, if not all, Third World writers have to arrive at this theoretical juncture, and decide when and how to confront the eurocentric mythology of colonialism. In the case of Africa, writers discovered that eurocentric representative of their history and literature is a misrepresentation, portraying a primitive and unrecognized culture. Following the examples of Fanon, Nehurah, and Rodney, they embraced the process of decolonization and recreation. The scientist, writer, and diplomat, Davidson Abioseh Nicol, from Sierra Leone, explained why he wrote: "because I found that most of those who wrote about us seldom gave any nobility to their African characters unless they were savages or servants or facing impending destruction. I knew differently."[5] In fact, some writers, in reading European literature, once found themselves on the side of the colonizer. In an interview with Bill Moyers, Achebe revealed his enlightenment at the university of Ibadan: "I suddenly saw that these books had to be read in a different light. Reading *Heart of Darkness*, for instance, which was a very highly praised book and which is still highly praised, I realized that I was one of those savages jumping up and down on the beach. Once that kind of Enlightenment comes to you, you realize that someone has to write a different story."[6]

G.D. Killam records another incident of enlightenment in Achebe's life, similar to the above. Achebe's intention was to study medicine, but he switched to literature, when he was "prompted by a reading of Joyce Cary's depiction of Nigeria and Nigerian character in *Mister Johnson* (1939). Achebe's purpose in writing was to "set the record of Nigeria's [and by extension Africa's] encounter with colonial history straight, to write about his own people and for his own people."[7]

On the other hand, the colonies could not totally depend on colonized writers to represent them because these writers could not survive or grow when the publishers, critics, promoters, and editors are the colonizers. (Rodney 212) Implied in this point is the unique complication facing Third World writers, which is what I intend to discuss in this paper. I will demonstrate how these writers respond to their complex situation of exploitation, marginalization, slavery, betrayal, indentureship, the hallmark of their strength. I shall limit my discussion to writers from Africa, India, and the English speaking Caribbean, since they have similar colonial experiences, and, for the most, were under the same colonial master.

Terry Eagleton's post-marxist analysis of colonized writers' predicament supports Rodney's point.[8] However, Eagleton advances his analysis to demonstrate an important facet about these writers; that is Marxist criticism also focuses on:

> The means of literary production, distribution and exchange in a particular society—how books are published, the social composition of their authors and audiences, level of literacy, the social determinants of 'taste.' It also examines literary texts for their 'sociological' relevance, raiding literary works to abstract from them themes of interest to the social historian. (2)

Such an approach provides a better understanding and appreciation of the enormous task facing the Third World writers, by demonstrating the terribleness of the socio-economic and political conditions of Africa, India, and the Caribbean under which these writers progress. These conditions include language implication, the past, system of evaluation, effects of colonial criticism, and betrayal by politicians.

A brief overview reveals that Africa was colonized by the British, French, and Portuguese for a period of fifty years. India was colonized by the British for two hundred years, while the West Indies was under slavery for just over a hundred years and under British colonization for another hundred years. Viney Kirpal in "Fiction of the 'Third World' in English," provides an insightful overview of colonialism in the Third World:

> Colonization stretching over three to four centuries in the "third world" countries—in special in the Africas, India, and in the West Indies—has affected the native's sensibility. On the credit side, colonization has modernized these societies—introduced new modes of production, introduced a system of liberal education that has helped the native to question traditional, authoritarian, superstition-ridden modes of thought, introduced him to an alternative, liberal religion. On the debit side, the colonizers consciously worked to break the spirit of rebellion against British rule by "educating" the native "suitably" and by engendering an inferiority complex and difference in him vis-a-vis his own culture and traditional values. As a result, though he belongs to countries that are independent today, the native still tends to look up to his former rulers for general guidance, monetary assistance, technical advice and intellectual lead so that ironically enough, the

economic-political equation between the former and the latter remains what it was in the days of British subjugation.[9]

Even though Kirpal's credit side of colonialism is debatable, her comment clearly indicates that the effects of colonialism still haunt the Third World. The colonizers have hung 'an albatross' around the neck of the Third World, and release comes only from telling the story.[10] This is the task of Third World writers who must first excavate the rubbish and rubble laying at their feet before they can build a discovering and defining body of literature.[11]

On the socio-economic and political front, Third World countries "have failed to confront the problems of poverty, unemployment, overpopulation, hunger, illiteracy and disease," while "the native rulers have only replaced the foreign ruler—the distance between the leaders and the masses having strongly underlined the fact that even after independence nothing has changed for the common man." (Kirpal 77) Corruption, betrayal, imprisonment, senseless killing and assassination, rape, and dictatorship have dominated many of these countries, especially countries in Africa. As a result of this unhealthy state in the Third World, growth and development are curtailed, the natives feel trapped, and they resort to different forms of escape and escapism. These themes surface in the works of many Third World writers,[12] but Naipaul's *Miguel Street* and Errol John's *Moon on a Rainbow Shawl* best illustrate them. Laban Erapu points out that the stories and characters of *Miguel Street* are linked together by "the similar destiny of seemingly inevitable disillusionment in which they all wind up."[13] Erapu further indicates that this disillusionment "builds up the pattern of the whole novel, which ends on a similar note as the disillusioned narrator makes his own escape to a larger world than the limited and limiting Miguel Street. Thus escape by the end becomes the main theme." (xii) To this effect, Kirpal points out that "Colonization has meant not just geographic-political occupation or economic plunder of today's 'third world' but also a spiritual and moral stunting of the native's character and confidence that has left him incapacitated to meet the challenges of running a country independently." (77) This "spiritual and moral stunting of the native's character and confidence" is reflected in the narrator's departure from Miguel Street: "I left them all and walked briskly towards the aeroplane, not looking back. Looking only at my shadow before me, a dancing dwarf on the tarmac." (222) Commenting on this closing metaphor in *Miguel Street,* Erapu indicates that the "dancing dwarf" reflects "the narrator's view of himself at the departure and the life he leaves behind." (xx) Erapu further links the fate of the narrator to that of the Third World: "Like the other people he has lived among, in the end the gruelling life and environment of Miguel Street has drained him and reduced him to size. This, one feels, is the author's view of the life in an emergent society in the Third World as he expresses it in a later novel, *The Mimic Men."* (xx)

The African situation includes apartheid, segregation, racial discrimination, inequality, injustice and exploitation, instability of regimes, and endless coups d'etat.[14] These socio-economic and political problems, apart from affecting each other, cause tremendous implications for African writers and critics. They create unsafe, uncertain, and unwholesome conditions under which these writers have to work. And in so doing they disrupt the process of continuity and building. Johnson remarks: "Socio-economic problems, in terms of the growth and development of society, are the most pressing pre-occupations of a nation as they could easily affect the political climate and change the course of the society's historical evolution." (132) Furthermore, African writers have to contend with a frightening scenario which Claire L. Dehon describes as follows: "An unprecedented growth in population accompanied by poor management accelerated desertification; a depressed economic situation plagues many countries; heads of state and their cohorts are in many instances all-powerful, tyrannical, and more personal in their own enrichment that in the welfare of their people; intellectual and businessmen are emigrating to the West, frustrated by the living and working conditions in their own countries."[15] Dehon further points out that African writers encounter direct problems to their writing process. Such problems include the material aspects of writing: "the high price of stationery, the luxury of a typewriter, and the lack of proper accommodations conducive to literary activities"; the economic problem which includes few publishing houses and high prices of texts[16]; and, politics: "no African government permits freedom of speech as we understand it in the West." Censureship is reinforced with punishment such as loss of jobs, houses, and reputations, while due process depends on the will of officials, their whims, their familial or tribal ties and bribes. Government control over education manifests in selection of texts for high schools by government officials, while professors's selections are monitored. Governments own the newspapers, publishing houses, and radio and television stations: "a circumstance that enables them to impose their concept of what a good book is and what it should contain." (8-9) Such dictatorial behavior is worse than colonialism, and African writers have to creatively devise ways of dealing with these destabilizing forces.

Additionally, in South Africa, apartheid with all its racial, discriminatory, and oppressive features has confronted writers with a different set of more complicated circumstances. Now, the socio-economic and political changes, the so-called dismantling of apartheid, present new challenges for these writers, who have become "sensitive to the events of racial discrimination, segregation, inequality, injustice, and exploitation." (Johnson 130)

The central question for these writers is what approach would best serve themselves and their countries in post-independence as they seek to continue the process of decolonization. These writers recognize and realize the importance of literature in throwing off the colonial burden. Edward Said postulates the role of literature in the process of decolonization: "For in the decades-long struggle to achieve decolonization and independence from European control, literature has played a crucial role in the re-establishment of a national cultural heritage, in the re-instatement of native idioms, in the re-imagining and re-figuring of local histories, geographies, communities. As such then literature not only mobilized active resistance to incursions from the outside but also contributed massively as the shaper, creator, agent of illumination within the realm of the colonized."[17]

This awareness of the importance of literature is the responsible factor for Achebe's writing career. Simon Gikandi, specialist in Achebe's studies, argues that "Achebe's seminal status in the history of African literatures lies precisely in his ability to have realized that the novel provided a new way of reorganizing African cultures, especially in the crucial juncture of transition from colonialism to national independence." (30-31) In fact, all Third World writers possess this consciousness, whether they use their writing as a decolonizing tool or not, and they participate in the process in different ways.[18] Srinivas Iyengar sees the role of literature as "The means of giving form and utterance to the despairs and hopes, the enthusiasm and apathy, the thrill of joy and the stab of pain—all the vicissitudes in fact—of a nation's history as it moves from freedom to slavery, from slavery to revolution, from revolution to independence, and again from independence to the tasks of reconstruction which involve further experience of futility and failure."[19]

So, literature for the Third World writers becomes not only an art, but a tool, a weapon, a guide, a teacher,[20] and a prophet. As a teacher, for instance, literature has to re-educate the natives of former colonies. In his essay, "The Novelist as Teacher," Achebe illustrates the story of his wife's pupil who, when asked why he "wrote about winter when he meant the harmattan," replied that he did not want the other boys to call him "a bushman." Achebe proceeded to point out that his role as a writer is "to teach that boy that there is nothing disagraceful about the African weather, that the palm-tree is a fit subject for poetry," and in so doing he will help his "society regain belief in itself" thus eradicating "the complexes of the years of denigration and self-abasement." (44)

In 1972 Camara Laye echoed a similar purpose of reversing the destructive work of colonialism through the education of his literature. Laye notes the purpose of his positive literary portrayal: "In showing the beauty of this culture, my novel testifies to its greatness. People who had not been aware that Africa had its own culture were able to grasp the significance of our past and our civilization. I believe that this understanding is the most meaningful contribution of African literature."[21] In similar awareness, Kofi Awoonor, Ghanaian poet, novelist, and essayist takes Laye's point about the role of literature to another dimension by pointing out the double-edged role of the writer of such literature. He indicates that a Third World writer must be shaped by the society he is writing about, and he must shape the society he is writing for: "An African writer must be a person who has some kind of conception of the society in which he is living and the way he wants the society to go."[22]

Mulk Raj Anand sees the novel as a central tool for emancipation. He sums up the Third World situation which gives rise to the writing motivation: "We have the struggle against slavery of mind and body of those who cannot bear the responsibility of freedom and accept subservience after periods of struggle for liberty."[23] The Indian writer proceeds to advocate the writers' role in such an oppressed condition:

> In the struggle for the novel of the new consciousness, of new heroes and heroines, new situations and new passions, we might accept the fact that everything changes, an ever fresh light has to be thrown on the lives of individuals revealing many obscure references, unsuspected by the naive, or even the sophisticated readers. I am, then, for a flood of novels, of the new consciousness in our new cultural awakening. (12)

Anand is for "a flood of novels," but he is for a certain type of novel, which deals with the real, present, new world, unlike his contemporary, R.K. Narayan's emphasis on the past, old, and philosophic world where characters endure their suffering as an inevitable punishment of past crimes and as a right response for a better, future life. Further, Anand deals with the real world of love, hate, pride, war, oppression, injustice, and exploitation where characters must respond to situations and change them.

Such perspective and pursuit of literature permit Anand to fix Third World writers into two major categories. In the first category, "narrative assumes the form of the literature of pleasure" because these writers "put down their remembrances, and achieve a beauty of expression," in order to "contemplate the inner and outer currents of their lives in flow." (8-9) Such writers include Narayan, Walcott, and Achebe. In the second category, "the more dynamic urges come through the quest of self in the workaday world" producing the "literature of truth, based on the experience of the struggle to be, to do, and to possess." (8-9) Writers in the second category include Wole Soyinka, Ngugi wa Thiong'o, George Lamming, Alex La Guma, Athol Fugard, and Anand himself. Writers like Wilson Harris, V.S. Naipaul, and Jean Rhys can be placed in both categories.

K.R. Shirwadkar argues that "the major experimental trend that informs Third World fiction is the struggle of human beings for betterment of communal life either by preservation of traditional order or by progress towards new order."[24] This base creates a superstructure of frustration and occasionally fulfillment. For example, African fiction portrays "a sense of frustration in different shades often in a sense of self identity before and the sense of disillusion after independence." (46) This sense of despair results from political corruption and betrayal in post-independent Africa. Even the prolific Caribbean writer, Naipaul, portrays pessimism and hopelessness because of similar conditions in the Caribbean. *Miguel Street, A House for Mr. Biswas, The Mimic Men,* and *The Guerrillas* emphatically illustrate Third World frustration. (48) Naipaul remarks in *The Middle Passage:* "History is built around achievement and creation; and nothing was created in the West Indies."[25]

Indian fiction demonstrates less frustration and despair. Raja Rao and R.K. Narayan employ philosophy and humour to depict a sense of fulfillment, but Anand echoes some of the Third World's frustration and despair especially in his works *Coolie, The Village,* and *Untouchable.* (Shirwadkar 48-50) However, on the whole, writers from the three colonized territories experience and express various degrees of disillusionment. And this difference is partly due to the different nature of their colonial experiences, as well as their different religious philosophies. Africa and India have been ruptured by slavery and indentureship respectively, then colonization, while the Caribbean has been the converging field of slavery, indentureship, and colonization. Shirwadkar's comparative overview of this situation is useful, for while portraying the "traumatic experience" of the Third World, he also differentiates the responses of the writers: "Achebe, Soyinka, Okara,

Ngugi, Naipaul and others have communicated the deep sense of frustration brought about by the disintegration of the old order as well as the confusion and moral anarchy created by the new order. The end of colonialism and the consequential illusions and disillusions were a traumatic experience for the sensibility and consciousness of the Third World. The Africans saw the future dark and the Caribbean turned cynical. However, in India, the novelist retained faith and hope even after failure or defeat." (50)

African literature responds most passionately to colonialism and post-independence. It confronts corruption and oppression "with an intensity unique in aesthetic formulation of form and feeling, demanding express commitment from the writer."[26] On one hand, these writers have to deal with the effects of colonization: "Black writers reasoned that Africa's dignity and values, which were felled by the sword of westernized invaders, must be recovered by the pen of the . . . Africans."[27] On the other hand, they have to contend with post-independent African leaders. Achebe, Soyinka, Ngugi, Aluko, and other African writers are dissatisfied with the new rulers of Africa because of political corruption and betrayal.

According to V. Panduranga Rao, Ngugi exploits "a largely personalized narrative mode" to present "his characteristically African reaction to the damaging effects of the colonial encounter and the neo-colonial hang-over on the psychological setup of a common Gikuyu man." (132) Ngugi, like Soyinka, sees the writer as the "conscience of the nation,"[28] and from this perspective, he declares a universal humanitarian role for the writers:

> It is not enough for the African artist, standing aloof, to view society and highlight its weakness. He must try to go beyond this, to seek out the sources, the causes and the trends. . . . All over the world the exploited colored majority, from the Americans, across Africa and the Middle East, to the outer edges of Asia, is claiming its own. The artist in his writings is not exempted from the struggle. By diving into the sources, he can give moral direction and vision to a struggle which, though suffering temporary reaction, is continuous and is changing the face of the twentieth century.[29]

Like Soyinka and other writers, Ngugi sees the role of the writer/artist as a "courageous act and correcting force" in Third World corruption, but while he stresses a Marxist approach which necessitates the struggle of the masses, Soyinka ignores the masses. (Killam 5-11)

Soyinka is not only upset with the political leaders of post-independent Africa, he is "particularly incensed with the hypocrisy of religious leaders and with the ineffectuality and sheer apathy of the intellectuals." (Ngugi, "Satire in Nigeria" 62) Brother Jero, in *Trials of Brother Jero*, represents the religious and political leaders who selfishly "profit themselves at the expense of the masses." (63) His speech illustrates how he keeps his followers dissatisfied to ensure a dependence-syndrome:

> I am glad I got here before any customers—I mean worshippers—well, customers if you like. I always get that feeling every morning that I am a shop-keeper waiting for customers. The regular ones come at definite times. Strange, dissatisfied people. I know they are dissatisfied because I keep them dissatisfied. Once they are full, they won't but I won't let him. If I do, he will become contented, and then that's another of my flock gone forever. (211)

Soyinka's satirical rebuke is not only for the political and religious leaders, but also for "the intellectual class in Nigeria," the "academic gentlemen in their university ties and gowns." Soyinka scorns these intellectuals because of their compromise with corruption, seeing them "as having neglected their rightful role of speaking out for the truth. Instead, they either approve the status quo, rationalizing away its corruption or else they condone it by their silence." (Ngugi, "Satire" 63-64) In "A Dance of the Forests," only the court poet raises his voice, prophet-like, against the evil of the king and his "whorish queen." (68-69)

Soyinka ridicules the academicians in sexual terms by portraying them as effeminate, westernized, and sterile. (66) The best example of Soyinka's attack on the intellectuals is Lakunle' in *The Lion and the Jewel*, the "middle-headed sloganeering,"[30] and "cowardly braggart" whose "culturedness consists of his opposition to the bride price," and who dreams of "dance-halls where even old women can learn the waltz and fox-trot, and . . . learn to kill like christians and other educated people." (Ngugi, "Satire" 66)

Achebe also rebukes the intellectuals. His novel, *No Longer at Ease,* depicts the tragedy of a scholar, Obi, whose eurocentric and materialistic life style forces him to succumb to bribery and corruption, resulting in his downfall. But Achebe's handling of post-independent corruption and betrayal is more delicate and philosophic. He recognizes that the world holds many problems for the colonized people, and he sees literature as one of the ways available to the colonized writer "to organize himself and his society to meet the perils of living." (qtd. Gikandi 31) "The perils of living" have been forced upon colonized people by the colonizer when a false reality was handed down to them. He believes that art becomes the means by which colonized people can create a new order of reality for themselves. (*Hopes and Impediments* 95-96) Such strong "belief that narrative can indeed propose an alternative world beyond the realities imprisoned in colonial and pre-colonial relations of power" motivates his pursuit of a postcolonial aesthetic, which advocates that "fiction allows the writer to express an alternative order of things to the realities framed by imperialism and western domination." (Gikandi 31)

Comparatively different to Africa, "the Indian literary scene remains more sedate, secure and sultry." (Bhatnagar 32) The effects of colonization subtly create two streams of writing. One includes "a unified fervour, passion and devotion to one's country and culture," while the other includes "dissipated withdrawal in self-criticism, promoting irony, satire and caricature in the pre- and post-independence literature respectively." (33) The complement of these two categories, like the complement of Anand and Narayan, provides a complete picture of India. Anand is "a novelist of the working class," while Narayan is "a novelist of the middle class."[31] Conscious of his Western audience, Narayan selects "aspects of reality" which enhance his comic treatment. (141) This is why Naipaul claims that Narayan portrays an unreal India.[32] But Anand focuses on the proletariats. He "deals with the misery and wretchedness of the poor and their struggle for a better life." (Verghese 126) In *Apology for Heroism*, Anand declares: "as my media as a writer were the memory and imagination, and the substance of my work became the whole of my varied experience, the theme of my work became the whole man and the whole gamut of human relationship, rather than only one single part of it." (78) His ultimate objective is to teach people, through his writings, "to recognize the fundamental principles of human living and exercise viligance in regard to the real enemies of freedom and socialism." (91) His writings also aim at raising "the untouchables, the peasants, the serfs, the coolies, and the other suppressed members of society, to human dignity and self-awareness in view of the abjectness, apathy and despair in which they are sunk." (93)

Caribbean socio-economic, historical and political past complicates its "fabric of divisions and diversities." (Bhatnager 30) Because of its mixture of people from Africa,[33] India,[34] and Europe[35] there is a uniquely diverse composition of personalities and approaches. Dolly Zulakha Hassan describes the West Indian society as one "made up of different peoples—an amalgam of whites, blacks, East Indians, Chinese, Portuguese, mixed races, and in Jamaica, Jews and Lebanese—uprooted and displaced from their original cultures."[36] V.S. Naipaul uses a universal approach to correct and rebuild the Caribbean through his satire, sarcasm, irony, and humour. Along with the above, he employs caricature in presenting the "complex fate of the Caribbean," while Wilson Harris, John Hearne, George Lamming, Andrew Salkey, and Samuel Selvon pursue the rebuilding of the native's cultural image, (Bhatnager 30-31) and each uses different techniques. Derek Walcott focuses on the socio-political, economic, and cultural struggle which results from the Caribbean cultural pluralism. Walcott's artistic and dramatic approach incorporates his mulatto metaphor to depict the freshness and uniqueness of the Caribbean, while Edward Braithwaite uses a historical and poetic approach that has been emersed in afrocentricism to advance the theory of knowing your history in order to find your identity and to achieve your destiny. Lamming uses a Marxist approach to focus on the working class who, he believes, will overthrow the oppressors. Michael Anthony forces his readers to look at the Caribbean from a different point of view, and then he asks about the future of postcolonial Caribbean.

The historical and cultural diversity influences the writers' thematic and stylistic diversity, and this becomes the strength of these writers. For example, Naipaul's cynical and negative portrayal of the Caribbean's development finds its opposite and complement in Walcott's creative and positive portrayal. Naipaul postulates in *A Bend in the River:* "The world is what it is; men who are nothing, who allow themselves to become nothing, have no place in it."[37] This follows a similar note in his famous statement in *The Middle Passage* that "nothing was created in the West Indies," (29) as well as it links with the displacement of his characters. But Walcott rejects such a pessimistic view of the Caribbean by counter-acting that "if there was nothing, there was everything to be made. With this prodigious ambition one began." ("What the Twilight Says" 4) Cynically, Naipaul may reply, building what? The thing Popo builds? "The thing without a name?" (*Miguel Street* 17-25) Yet such diverse perspectives do enhance the growth of Caribbean literature, as well as world literature. Robert Hammer perceives that "although the two [Naipaul and Walcott] take opposite positions on crucial issues, they are actually complementary and necessary to each other in rendering a complete picture of the West Indies."[38] The same can be said about the opposition between Walcott and Lamming, Achebe and Soyinka, or Ngugi, Anand and Narayan, and other Third World writers.

(b) Confrontation of history/past

One of the central questions is how do these writers confront their past of slavery, indentureship, war, loss, and colonial exploitation. In the case of South Africa it includes dealing with the effects of apartheid. With their diversity in approaching any issue, one observes a distinctive dichotomy which I call the traditional versus the modern. In Africa, there is no easy way out of the conflict caused by the clash of two vastly different cultures as a result of colonialism. In Soyinka's *The Lion and the Jewel*, Baroka's (the Bale's) hard-headed conservatism and sexual exploitations of women do not offer much hope for change and progress, but placed against (the alternative) Lakunle's half-baked and unformed values, representative of the new postcolonial society which is neither African nor European, the Bale wins the Jewel, Sidi. (Jones 47) On the contrary, in Achebe's *Things Fall Apart,* traditional Umuofia molds Okonkwo to see his father's artistic life as a failure and to resist such a life. The culture promotes competition; achievement; gaining of titles, wives and fame; and tribal class. Okonkwo, who lives with fear of failing like his father and of being called weak, strives to achieve as much as possible, and becomes a prisoner of the laws. For example, he beats his wife, shoots at another of his wives, helps to murder Ikemefuna, is exiled, opposes colonization, and commits suicide. But compared to modern European society, Umuofia is still a strong society, and in several ways better. However, colonization has raped this African society through imposition of modern technology on a traditional culture. This imposition results in the displacement of Africans living in a conflicting society.

In India also there is no easy way out of the effects of British colonialism. Narayan advocates traditional India as against modern India since capitalistic approach of modern, technological India exploits and dehumanizes the Indian people. Such an approach is self-destructive. For example, in *The Guide,* Railway Raju's compassionate liberation of Rosie from her slavish and patriarchal marriage causes him to rise to fame and prosperity, but his exploitation and manipulation of Rosie's, now renamed Nalini, dancing career causes his fall and imprisonment. He destroys himself as he tries to fulfill a forced religious role. Similarly, in *Vendor of Sweets,* Jagan's victory and peace in religious retreat from the hostility of his son Mali's westernized approach to business is a better option than Mali's modern, self-destructive life-style. Mali becomes cruel and self-centered as he plunges into corruption and destruction as seen through his marriage, business, and imprisonment. Further, Narayan, in *The Man Eater of Malgudi,* juxtaposes the self-destruction of the bullying taxidermist, Vasu, with the triumph of artist/printer, Nataraj.

Anand's solution to India's problem is the opposite of Narayan's answer. He uses Bakha, the central character of *Untouchable,* to eliminate western christianity and Gandhi's religious non-violence as possible answers to the oppression and discrimination caused by India's caste/class system. He advocates the "flush system," a modern technological device to eradicate human waste, thus dispensing with the inhumanity of the sweepers' job.

In the Caribbean, George Lamming and Derek Walcott advocate a combination of traditional and modern, yet each approach is vastly different. Lamming argues in *In the Castle of My Skin,* that a denial of history leads to the loss of identity. The villagers do not want to hear about past slavery. This is why they have no clearly defined path for the future (postcolonialism) after ownership of land is passed from the British landlord to the new elite of the working class, Mr. Slime and others. The result is another form of slavery or colonialism. Displacement steps in as Pa is placed in a nursing home, and others are scattered elsewhere. In fact the text suggests that a combination of the perspectives of Ma and Pa (old) and Trumper and the Narrator (young) is needed to guide the villagers out of the betrayal of a new middle class exploitation.

Walcott uses himself, a mulatto, as a central metaphor to depict the Caribbean's problem and solution. A merging of his African and European heritage, in *Another Life,* is needed to deal with the rubbish of slavery and colonialism. Along this line of interpretation, *Ti-Jean and His Brothers* becomes an allegory to depict unsuccessful and successful methods of dealing with the force of evil, the colonizer. Gross-Jean, representative of violent rebellion, fails because the white master possesses force and tools of strength. Mi-Jean, representative of the attempt to master the white man's book-learning in order to beat him with his own method of oppression, also fails because the white man constantly 'fixes' his educational system to be used as a tool to oppress the colonies. Ti-Jean, representative of a combination of indigenous tradition and modern tact, defeats the oppressor/planter/devil. Ti-Jean's dependence on his mother and the forest creatures, and the use of his intelligence and force secures his victory and life for the unborn Bolom, giving birth to the Caribbean future. The success is the triumph of the small man or little people.

(c) Colonial Criticism

Another major complication facing Third World writers is colonial criticism.[39] Criticism can break or make a writer. It has the power to create or destroy. For the most part, colonial criticism has accomplished the destructive function on colonized writers. When it comes to the relationship between Third World literature and the colonizer's canon, Wilentz's comment provides a useful understanding: "To examine Caribbean writers who write in English in relation to the British canon we must understand the basic tenets of this canon—that of colonialism and cultural domination."[40] There must be the poor for the rich to get richer; there must be the colonized for the colonizer to increase; there must be the excluded for the canon to enjoy power and prestige. Therefore, we must also understand that "beneath the disinherited procedures of literary judgement and discrimination can be discerned the out-lines of other, harsher words: exclusion, subjugation, dispossession."[41] Decades of oppression, discrimination, hostility and domination have left coloured writers with an uphill task of self-discovery and self-definition for themselves and their people in the midst of colonial criticism. Although the colonizers have retreated from their positions of control in many colonies, they have continuously pursued opportunites to assert their authority over people of colour. Hoyt Fuller's point, though used in the context of the Black and White controversy in America, serves to illustrate my point:

> But the White Literary Establishment is not willing to release its stranglehold on black literature. It has been traditional, of course, that white critics decided what was valuable and valid in black literature. Robert A. Bone, for one, has been floating along for years on a reputation as the leading "authority" on black literature on the basis of his book, *The Negro Novel in America.* In most academic circles, Mr. Bone cannot be challenged by a black writer or critic; his judgement is final, his taste is infallible.[42]

According to Nick Aaron Ford, Bone and the "Protestant-Anglo-Saxon oriented critics" condemn the protest novel for its propaganda, because it deals with race, but praise the propanganda in novels by Charles Dickens, Sinclair Lewis, Norman Mailer, Theodore Dreiser, Ernest Hemingway, and John Steinbeck because their words do not include race.[43] Although the most significant novels of the past are remembered for their focus on moral and social issues, "any novel by a Black writer which deals honestly and effectively with the problems of race without attempting to blunt the cutting edge by sublimating it into the larger context of universality is denied serious critical attention in obedience to the strictures of aestheticism." (61)

The relationship between Third World literature and multiculturalism is reciprocal. Third World literature enhances multiculturalism, while multiculturalism provides voice for volumes of Third World literature that have been marginalized and silenced by the traditional literary canon. This provision of voice to an excluded literature further ensures the presence of diversity which is the hallmark of Third World literature. But an elitist group of criticism has threatened to destroy the emergence of this literature. For example, the youngesst body of literature emerging out of colonialism faced this threat.[44] In the late 1960s several prominent literary critics warned West Indian writers and literary community about the "dangers inherent in allowing external perceptions to dominate the evaluation of West Indian literature."[45] The greatest danger rested on the fact that the colonizer-colonized relationship dictated the relationship between British critics and West Indian writers. These critics became "patronizing and simplistic" towards the writers, (26) but the imperialist agenda almost succeeded in crippling Caribbean literature. Allis further illustrates how "British critics writing in the popular press—*The London Times, London Sunday Observer, Times Literary Supplement, New Statesman, Spectator,* and *Listener*—approached this new literature from a similarly benign point of view." (26) British reviews and criticism viciously attacked Caribbean writers's language, style, content, characterization, and even their presence in London.

Caribbean literature came to the United States of America from London, and white American reviews of the fifties and sixties "showed a tendency to regard West Indian writers as naive and incapable of grasping the significance of their subject matter." (31) African-American reviews initially attacked Caribbean writers on the basis of racial alliance. A 1972 review in *Freedomways* notes that George Lamming's "*Natives of My Person* is rendered in a language and style that are simply too European to excite the interest of readers who are pretty turned-off by the symbols of white culture." (qtd. in Allis 34)

These colonial critics, described by Jomo Kenyatta as "professional friends and interpreters of the African" are people "who acquire a most proprietorial air when talking of the part of Africa they have happened to visit; they carve a personal sphereof influence and champion the most reactionary and the most separatist cause of whichever group among whom they happen to live. They are again most vehement in pointing out the unique intelligence, amiability and quick will of their adopted areas and groups." They are like the Commissioner in Achebe's *Things Fall Apart* applying critical theory to Obierika's narrative, representative of Third World writing. Obierika's "voice trembled and choked his words" which could only say to the Commissioner: "That man was one of the greatest men in Umuofia. You drove him to kill himself; and now he will be buried like a dog." (187) Although painful emotion over his friend Okonkwo's suicide would allow him to speak only a few words, yet in those few words he has declared a true and holistic perspective of the whole matter. He has summed up the entire tragedy of Okonkwo, Africa, and all colonized people. But the colonial critic, the Commissioner, a man of written language, will write a chapter, or a paragraph and still miss the point. Furthermore, Okonkwo's tragedy is insignificant to his selfish design or theme:

> In the book which he planned to write he would stress that point. . . . The story of this man who had killed a messenger and hanged himself would make interesting reading. One could almost write a whole chapter of him. Perhaps not a whole chapter but a reasonable paragraph, at any rate. There was so much else to include, and one must be firm in cutting out details. He has already chosen the title of the book, after much thought: *The Pacification of the Primitive Tribes of the Lower Niger.* (187)

From Cecil Abrahams's perspective the District Commissioner "is completely ignorant of the tumultuous event which had just occurred in the village." (2) Yet he has a superior attitude to the Africans. Intellectually, he feels that his perspective of the situation transcends the thoughts of "these primitive people." Achebe recognizes this "big-brother arrogance" in the colonialist critic who "sees the African writer as a somewhat unfinished European who with patient guidance will grow up one day and write like every other European, but meanwhile must be humble, must learn all he can and while at it give due credit to his teachers in the form of either direct praise or, even better since praise sometimes goes bad and becomes embarrassing, manifest self-contempt." ("Colonialist Criticism" 3)

In the whole process of colonial criticism, Third World literature and writers seemed to have been in a state of limbo: "a kind of nebulous territory whose inhabitants are in a constant state of uncertainty . . . a state of suspense, a state of doubt which does not allow comfort because nothing can be taken for granted," because the writer's history, culture, politics, writing, role, audience, language, "everything shifts, changes, upsets."[47] However, although critics like Kirpal Singh believe that Third World writers are still in limbo, their beliefs are far from the truth. Today, there is a continuously rising tide of criticism from Third World scholars which has counter-acted the narrow, negative criticism from the colonialists. This body of criticism has liberated the minds of Third World people, and has taken the writers out of any negative limbo. If they are in any limbo, it is a positive one where they use their complex circumstances to portray an enriched diversity resulting in the uniqueness of these writers. And Singh's comment provides the rationale for one to see the uniqueness and diversity which Third World writers bring to all literatures: "The Third World writer is a very complex and complicated individual, a composite of many variables, a product of conflicting trends and possibilities." (71)

(d) Language Controversy

One of the most controversial baggage of colonialism is language which presents Third World writers with numerous complexities. M.J. Fenwick points out that "one of the most devastating effects of colonization has been the fragmentation of the region into the separate languages of the colonizers."[48] The language areas include Spanish-speaking, French-speaking, Dutch-speaking, and English-speaking nations. Fenwick further explains that such "categorization denies a legitimate place to literature in Creole, Patois, Papiamento, Scranan-Tongo, Hindi, Urdu, and to literature written in indigenous languages still active in parts of Central America," and it "denies integrity to the rich synthesis of cultures—Amerindian, African, Middle Eastern, Asian, and European—which are the Caribbean area." (xiii)

The colonizers's languages, namely English, French, Dutch, Spanish, and Portuguese, went wherever they plundered and pillaged. In the case of the British, English developed rapidly because of their colonial expansion in Asia, Africa and the West Indies. Narsu K. Nihalani illustrates the politics of the expansion of the English language: "English which was just a minor language in the sixteenth century, has come to attain the unique position of a world language today."[49] The writer points out that contrary to popular argument, the reasons for this development are non-linguistic; rather, they are political: "Sure enough, the main reason for the world-wide expansion of English was colonization. It has rightly been said that language and power go together. The English language went wherever the Britishers went and established their colonies and empire." (39) Nihalani further explains that in British West Indies, English became the sole language although there were several dialects and the creolized form, whereas in Africa and India, English never became the dominant language, but has been used as a complementary language. (40)

Third World writers have been further marginalized on the basis of language. They have been denied the freedom of writing in the language of their love and choice by promotional, canonical, publication, and critical pressures. Even those who freely write in English, are expected to recreate the colonizer's English. Caliban must use Prospero's language because power dictates language. For until recently, many Third World nations were required to speak and write standard English, meaning British English, not only by the British, but also by Third World intellectuals who did their studies in England. The colonized were expected to use British grammatical structure, accent, and pronunciation. And even the badly spoken and written rural dialects of England were regarded as better language than our educated attempt of mimicking the British English. Nihalani points out that "the attitudes and reactions of the speakers of 'Mother English' to other Englishes in general and in the Third World Englishes in particular were far from those of tolerance, let alone recognition and acceptance. The speakers of British English were terribly arrogant and intolerant toward other Englishes." (40) Canonical marginalization reinforces colonial marginalization on the basis of language, and this is a plaguing issue to Third World writers. On one hand, these writers write for and about the natives, but on the other hand, they have to include a wider audience in order to earn a decent living and reputation. One cannot fault these writers for their inclusion of North American and European audiences since their governments cannot support them financially, and the reading audiences in their countries are small. In the Caribbean, for example: "the literary product is not a highly marketable commodity. West Indian literature is read by students in high school, in teachers' colleges and at the university; quite rarely is it read for pleasure or instruction by the relatively small percentage of literate people in our societies. It appears to be still true that the audience for West Indian literature is largely non-West Indian."[50]

Kenneth Ramchand provides useful insights on what he calls the "economic consequence." He claims that "until recently, West Indian books were priced strictly in relation to the purchasing power of the British buyer, and this invariably meant a price beyond the means of most West Indians in the islands."[51] Two key reciprocal factors emerge from the above point. In the first case, the reading audience grows slowly or decreases at times because of the high cost of books resulting from the unequal exchange rate. Presently, one British pound and one US dollar value 55.78 and 32 Jamaican dollars, 241.44 and 145 Guyanese dollars, 36.63 and 22 Nigerian neroes, 94.91 and 57 Kenyan shillings, and 53.28 and 32 Indian rupees respectively.[52] Is it therefore surprising and yet not surprising that in 1994 the 1992 Nobel Literature Prize winner, Derek Walcott's autobiographical *Another Life* is out of print? Other Caribbean works like Lamming's *In the Castle of My Skin* and

John's *Moon on a Rainbow Shawl* are also out of print.[53] This 'out of print' issue demonstrates the point that because of the exchange rate the growth of the reading audience in the Caribbean is too slow to compete with a fast pace economy. In the second case, consumption influences production. Ramchand explains: "The need to be intelligible to his market (the British reading public), and to explain his culture and society to foreign readers led the West Indian author to make modifications to the language and content of his manuscript that were not demanded by stylistic or other artistic concerns." (96)

In the following passage from Samuel Selvon's *An Island is a World*, observe the extent to which the author has to go in order to accommodate his foreign audiences with explanations:

> Jennifer called him to breakfast. She had made "buljol"—a West Indian dish of salted codfish, one of the poor man's items of diet. The fish is soaked until it loses its hardness, and broken up into small pieces. Or roasted and treated in the same way. It is served with olive oil and fresh tomatoes and onions, and avocado pears, if they are in season. There is a kind of bread called "hops" and the "buljol" is most enjoyable with it.
>
> This morning had bought an avocado pear from a passing Indian vendor. The pear had come from Grenada, an island about one hundred miles from Trinidad, which could be seen from the Chachachacre lighthouse on a clear day, looking through a telescope. The pear had seen boxed with scores of others, and shipped on a schooner. (qtd. Ramchand 97)

In the case of the Indian writers, the language controversy appears to be of a mild nature. When dealing with a civilization so "multifarious and so complex"[54] and one that is "a wounded old civilization that has at last become aware of its inadequacies and is without the intellectual means to move ahead," (Naipaul, *India* 9-10) C.D. Narasimhaiah's response becomes appropriate: "But English is the only language in which we are all able to speak to one another." (qtd. Pollard 35) Pollard points out that because India endured colonialism from the British for two centuries the effect is "internal and psychological." (38) This kind of effect is subtle, and it tends to delude scholarly visibility, but it places Indian writers in a "more complex and more sophisticated situation." (38-39) Raja Rao's statement serves to illuminate this subtle complexity that is not as visible as the African language problem:

> One has to convey in a language which is not one's own. One has

> to convey the various shades and omissions of a certain thought-movement that looks maltreated in an alien language. I use the word "alien," yet English is not really an alien language to us. It is the language of our intellectual make-up—like Sanskrit or Persian was before—but not of our emotional make-up. We are all instinctively bilingual, many of us writing in our own language and in English. We have grown to look at the large world as part of us. Our method of expression therefore has to be a dialect which will some day prove to be as distinctive and colorful as the Irish or the American. Time alone will justify it. (qtd. Pollard 38)

Rao's statement demonstrates "the paradox of a divided consciousness and a determined purpose side by side." (38) It reveals a struggle of the psyche that can be hidden from the natural eyes, but it is honest.

R.K. Narayan's approach to the language controversy is similar to Rao's. He uses a unique brand of English without focusing on any violent, visible complication. According to Peter Nazareth, "Narayan is popular in the West because he portrays Indians in a way which makes them understood by non-Indians," (156) whereas Mulk Raj Anand tries to explain Indians to the West. Nazareth further points out the effectiveness of Narayan's use of language:

> Instead of presenting these complex ideas in complex language, he presents them in the simple language. . . . Like his African counterpart, Narayan is faced with the problem of making his characters speak in English whereas they do not speak in English in real life. He solves this problem not by transliterating like Gabriel Okara, but by using a very simple kind of "primary school" English. (157-58)

The language controversy in Africa is of great magnitude and visibility. The central argument is whether African writers should use the colonizers' languages or the native languages. Is Caliban's mastery and use of Prospero's language a decolonizing act, or should he return to his own language? This debate has divided African writers to the point of bitterness and betrayal.

Eric Sellin points out that language, like economics, "is an arm of colonization."[55] It is the right arm of colonization because the colonial education required African students to acquire European languages as a "pre-requisite to the latter's [Africans] reaching a level of proficiency necessary for literary assimilation." (48) In fact, severe embarrassment and punishment were meted out to students who spoke their mother tongues. Ngugi notes that in 1952 after the declaration of a state of emergency in Kenya, all schools run by patriotic nationals were taken over by colonial regimes and placed under District Education Boards chaired by Englishmen, and English was the official language. It was humilating to speak Gikuyu in a school's vicinity. The culprit was given corporal punishment, three to five strokes of cane on his bare buttocks, or made to carry a metal plate around his neck with inscriptions such as "I am stupid," or "I am a donkey."[56] (*Decolonizing the Mind* 10-11) Summing up the entire African situation, Sellin cites that "every effort was made to impose French, Portuguese, or English language and to demean the native languages in Africa." (48)

The growth of African literature in the latter half of the twentieth century has depended heavily on the writers's use of European languages as well as European publication and promotion. Kitia Touré's response to my comment about the dependence of Caribbean writers on European promotion and audience reveals a similar situation in Africa. Touré noted that his first book received little or no promotion from France, and this resulted in the sale of no copies in Africa. However, his second book received favourable review and promotion in Europe, and this resulted in massive sales of his book in Africa.[57] This illustration clearly indicates that African writers' future, like that of other Third World writers, hinges on the colonizers' will.

To publish, to succeed, to reach large audiences, including their own, African writers, like other Third World writers, have to borrow language, and in some cases form, from the establishment. Sellin remarks that "taking the example from francophone literature we find that the early texts tended to adopt with a natural timidity—the ready made language which yet best conformed to the African writer's predilections." (54) Several critics including Eustace Palmer and Peter Nazareth have traced European writers' influence on African writers. For example, Thomas Hardy's influence can be seen in Achebe's works, while D.H. Lawrence and Joseph Conrad have influenced Ngugi. But as these writers become more knowledgeable of their history and more secured and established, they sever their dependence-link with their European promoters.

Such a stage resulted in the explosion of the language controversy when Ngugi not only decided to write in Gikuyu, but advocated that African writers should do the same. Ngugi declares that "African literature can only be written in African language, that is, the language of the African peasantry and working class, the major alliance of classes in each of our nationalities and the agency for the coming inevitable revolutionary break with neo-colonialism." (*Decolonizing the Mind* 27)

Ngugi's reasons for such a radical act of revolution includes the fact that the colonizer's language and literature are alienating the Africans from themselves, placing them with the colonizer, and discriminating against Africans who have not mastered English in schools. (12) Srinivas illustrates the impact of Ngugi's decision:

> In deciding to write in Gikuyu instead of English, he [Ngugi] revises significantly the political agenda of the African writers. Ngugi may not have succeeded in getting many writers to follow him: but his achievement may be in the undoubted fact that those who have questioned socio-economic dependence but not linguistic colonialism can, after his discussion of the politics of language, be no longer at ease. (103)

Indeed, African writers are no longer at ease in this area of controversy. They have allowed themselves to be burdened down with the guilt of language use. Egejuru Phanuel Akubueze has documented a dialogue with contemporary African writers with the following summary:

> The questions raised in the interviews and the responses to them show some of the fine and deeply rooted effects of colonialism which make absolute independence a near impossibility for the new nations of Africa. The writers are quite touchy and often defensive on most issues, as if to admit their dependence on the West amounts to a betrayal of trust. They are truly caught in a vicious circle vis-a-vis their objective to achieve total independence in aesthetic matter. (153)

The language controversy, in particular has left key African writers like Ngugi and Achebe 'bobbing and weaving' and 'jabbing and sparring' at each other. This dogmatic approach by Ngugi has divided African writers and has threatened to destroy the diversity of African literature. Furthermore, it has left writers like Achebe struggling with internal complication. Kirpal Singh points out how troubled Achebe is; "how conviction after conviction, belief after belief, has had to be modified because it became too stressful, too taut to adhere to without hurting the psyche." (74) Singh's comments, however, fail to demonstrate a critical appreciation for the multifaceted complexity of the problems facing the African writers who are caught between the old and the new, between Africa and Europe, and between native languages and European languages. For earlier, Achebe has pointed out the positive side of English usage. Speaking of colonialism, he declares: "But on the whole it did bring together many peoples that hither gone their several ways. And it gave them a language with which to talk to one another."[58] Later, in 1987, in an interview with Colleen Lowe Morna, Achebe, after admitting to the dichotomy between Ngugi and himself, remonstrated: "I have never undermined African languages. I have never said that African languages should die. On the contrary, I have said that in addition to whatever European metropolitan language history has imposed on us, and with which we are operating in the nation states that we have today, we must make sure that our various indigenous languages are preserved and developed." (47)

Unlike Singh, I interpret Achebe's modifications as signs of growth and flexibility. Achebe identifies himself as a Nigerian, African, and as a man of the world. Having lived in different cultures, his experiences shape a more open and holistic perspective. In a similar manner, many Third World writers' universal perspective shapes their approach to language. In an interview, V.S. Naipaul summed up his appraoch: "A man must write to report his whole response to the world." (qtd. Lyn 53) This does not mean that Achebe and other Third World writers, in striving for an international audience in an international language, would negate their native audiences and languages. Rather, this approach safeguards their works from becoming isolated. If this happens, who will then decolonize the mass of colonial literature about Africa and the rest of the Third World?

During the 1950s and 1960s a tremendous increase in "immensity and volume" of Caribbean literature became a flowing stream.[59] However, unlike the African situation, there is no major, visible language controversy. According to Pollard, the absence of controversy results from the fact that Caribbean writers have no choice but to use English, since they are far removed from their origins. (39) However, George Lamming views this language disruption from a positive perspective:

> An important question, for the English critic, is not what the West Indian novel has brought to English writing. It would be more correct to ask what the West Indian novelists have contributed to English reading. For the language in which these books are written is English—which, I must repeat—is a West Indian language; and in spite of the unfamiliarity of its rhythms, it remains accessible to the readers of English anywhere in the world.[60]

Lamming further uses a decolonized interpretation of *The Tempest* to demonstrate a new perspective; a perspective which "is demystified as an intellectual process that resituates the colonial writer as an active agent of decolonization."[61] From this new and appropriated perspective, there is no argument about Caribbean writers' use of the colonizer's language versus the use of native languages. Rather, these writers confidently and forcefully use English in their own way as a tool and weapon to carve out their destiny. These are the Calibans of the Caribbean who have pioneered the linguistic transformation of which Lamming claims: "The old blackmail of language simply won't work any longer. For the language of modern politics is no longer Prospero's exclusive vocabulary. It is Caliban's as well; and since there is no absolute from which a moral prescription may come, Caliban is at liberty to choose the meaning of this moment." (158)

Gay Wilentz points out that "unlike the former colonies in Africa or India . . . there was no language native to the Caribbean after the almost complete genocide of the Amerindians." (261) In her essay, "English is a Foreign Anguish," Wilentz illustrates "how Caribbean writers have disrupted the colonial language and adopted it as a language of opposition," (262) but she also alludes to the painful experience of these writers. For example, Wilson Harris postulates how he has disrupted and appropriated the colonizer's language:

> I am not at all engaged in a politics of protest against the language of the so-called imperialist master. History within my mixed antecedents, across conflicting generations, has brought the supreme blessing of a language I genuinely love. A living language is a medium for which one must be profoundly grateful.
>
> English in which I write my novels, is my native language not because of historical imposition or accident but because of numinous proportions that sustains originality within a living text.[62]

Having made such a bold comment it is not contradictory for Harris to admit to the subtle complexities facing the Caribbean writers. In a seminar, at the University of Texas, in 1982, Harris explained his anguish: "I had to unlearn what I had learned. I could not just write 'The river is dark; the tree is green.' One of the tasks that began to hurt me personally is how to write that." (qtd. Wilentz 268)

Because of many variations of vocabulary, rhythm, register, intonation, dialect, ideolect, slang, and jargon, different complexities arise in the use of English, especially when evaluation and approval come from the colonizer. Decades after independence in the English speaking Caribbean, students still have to prepare for exams at GCE 'O' and 'A' levels. These exams are set and marked by British examiners who live in

England.[63] Caribbean students have to write British standard English for the examiners who have little knowledge about the Caribbean. In some cases students may not be aware that some words are not standard English, but creolized versions of English. In other cases certain words may have different meanings in the different Caribbean territories as well as in England. In a similar manner, Caribbean writers' plight becomes a linguistic one. Their promotion, publication, and reception depend mainly on British and, of late, American editors, publishers, and critics. Therefore, they have to make conscious linguistic decisions to accommodate themselves, regional audience, and international audience. Jean D'Costa illustrates the dilemma facing the Caribbean writers:

> The [Caribbean] writer operates within a polydialectal continuum with a creole base. His medium, written language, belongs to the sphere of standardized language which exerts a pressure within his own language community while embracing the wide audience of international standard English. . . . If the writer is to satisfy himself, his local audience and that wider international audience, he must evolve a literary dialect which will meet the following: the demands for acceptability within and without his own community, and the pressure for authentic representation of the language culture of his own community.[64]

Most of the first generation of Caribbean writers are still affected by the switching complexities of slavery and colonization, during which time several territories experienced several cultures and languages—namely Dutch, Spanish, French, and English—from the colonizers.[65] Then the confluence of Africa, Europe, and India in the Caribbean produced not only physical and cultural mulattoes, but also linguistic mulattoes. Derek Walcott, a notable mulatto example, expresses this cultural and linguistic tension in "A Far Cry from Africa":

> I who am poisoned with the blood of both,
> Where shall I turn, divided to the vein?
> I who have cursed
> The drunken officer of British rule, how choose
> Between this Africa and the English tongue I love?
> Betray them both, or give back what they give?[66]

Walcott's linguistic tension is further demonstrated in his plays. Commenting on Walcott's linguistic dilemma in *Dream on Monkey Mountain,* Ismith Khan, a Caribbean writer, indicates that "none of his characters could possibly speak with the sophistication, the erudition and the poetry which are emulations of British standards. Since the writer is loathe to cut things out or throw things away, he twists, bends, and forces extraneous elements into the body of his work—he must have those lines even though they are in a language, meter, and rhythm totally alien to his characters and their lives."[67] Khan argues that "had the writer gone to the extreme end of the spectrum of West Indian dialect," the play would not have been understood by American and British audiences. Yet the cry of post-Independent Caribbean has been for literature that is "autonomous, nationalistic, and home-grown." But Walcott "has pigeonholed himself before he even begins." (149) This 'pigeonholing' of Walcott is the experience of most Caribbean writers "because no one writes for the bottom drawer." (152) Khan and several other Caribbean writers have dialect novels in their "bottom drawers" because of negative reactions from editors and publishers. (152)

Nevertheless, a stumbling block has become a stepping stone. Walcott's mastery of the English language in his poetry, plays, fiction, and criticism, to the point of being awarded the Nobel Prize for literature in 1992, is indicative of the language success of the other writers. Because of these writers' linguistic flexibility they can write for audiences across the world, including the Caribbean. And this ability affords them a unique language mastery. They have developed a language mastery in the face of shifting circumstances which is the "nature of cultural behaviour in the Caribbean creole continua," where a language shift becomes a behavioral shift, resulting in a meaning shift.[68] D'Costa further illustrates the intricacy of this language mastery by Caribbean writers:

> The [Caribbean] writer confronts in his own mind the array of possible language forms which arise at the bidding of any single notion he may wish to express. At this partially conscious level he must shift the mental events, emotions, and patterns of association within him such that the ideal balance of meaning may be achieved. This suggests a kind of language competence in which variation, code-switching and minimal shifting form a complete whole rather than clearly separated systems realizing themselves in different surface structures. ("The West Indian Novelist and Language" 256)

Third World writers should be free to write in whatever language(s) they choose to write. They have emancipated themselves and people from the slavery of colonization. Should they or others hand a 'colonial or canonical albatross' around their necks? Should they continue to fetch the burden of discrimination and oppression in new forms? I agree with Srinivas's argument that "the 'choice' of English or any other European or any other European language is a political one."[69] These writers have enough baggage of complexity to deal with. They should not add another from the language controversy. Rather, they should write freely in the language of their choice, for in so doing they will represent the diversity of their people's culture. In addition to the use of native languages and standard English, Third World writers should be free to use pidgin, creole, English of secondary school leavers and university graduates, and the different flavour of dialects, ideolects, and registers. Such freedom will encourage Third World writers to capture "the flavour of African life,"[70] Indian life, and Caribbean life. Indeed, they will capture the multi-linguistic and multicultural dimensions of the rich diversity of Third World literature. And to those who accuse Third World writers writing in English of betrayal, Kamala Das's, a well-known Indian poet writing in English, poem provides the perspective I advocate in this paper:

> I am Indian, very brown, born in
> Malabar, I speak three languages, write in
> two, dream in one. Don't write in English, they said,
> English is not your mother-tongue. Why not leave
> Me alone, critics, friends, visiting cousins,
> Everyone of you? Why not let me speak in
> Any language I like? The language I speak
> Becomes mine, mine alone. It is half English, half
> Indian, funny perhaps, but it is honest,
> It is as human as I am human, don't
> You see? It voices my joy, my longings, my
> Hopes, and it is as useful to me as cawing
> Is to crows or roaring to the lions, it
> Is human speech, the speech of the mind that is
> Here and not there, a mind that sees and hears and
> Is aware. . . . (qtd. Nihalani 43)

NOTES

1. Walter Rodney's own quest to pursue truth beyond false history from the colonizer led him to rewrite African history in *How Europe Underdeveloped Africa* (Washington D.C.: Howard Univ. Press, 1974) which provides several examples of misrepresentations of history, the paradoxes of underdevelopment. Rodney points out that "many parts of the world that are naturally rich are actually poor and parts that are not so well off in wealth of soil and sub-soil are enjoying the highest standards of living." (20)
2. Qtd. in Rodney, p. 22. Frederick Douglass and Harriet Jacobs have documented the gross misappropriation of scriptures by slave masters and the system to keep slaves in subjection to their masters. For example, Douglass notes that his master, Thomas Auld, after experiencing religion, would "tie up a lame young woman, and whip her with a heavy cowskin upon her naked shoulders, causing the warm red blood to drip; and, in justification of the bloody deed, he would quote this passage of Scripture—"He that knoweth his master's will, and doeth it not, shall be beaten with many stripes." (85-86) Similarly, Jacobs records how Rev. Pike would preach his sermons to keep the slaves in subjection to the masters. His text reads: "Servants, be obedient to them that are your masters according to the flesh, with fear and trembling, in singleness of heart, as unto Christ." (68) Pike would further threaten the slaves with God's judgement: "If you disobey your earthly master, you offend your heavenly Master." (69)
3. Throughout this study West Indies and Caribbean are used interchangeably: "The West Indies (formerly British West Indies), or the English-speaking Caribbean, consists of Jamaica; the Leeward Islands (St. Kitts, Nevis, Anguilla, Antigua, Montserrat, the British Virgin Islands); the Windward Islands (St. Vincent, LuSt. cia, Dominica, Grenada); Barbados; Trinidad and Tobago; Belize (formerly British Hunduras) and Guyana (formerly British Guiana). Guyana, although geographically in South America, is regarded as linguistically, socially, culturally, and politically West Indian." (Zulakha 1)
4. Edward Said, *Orientalism* (New York: Vintage, 1979), p. 240.
5. Qtd. in Chinua Achebe, "Colonialist Criticism," in *Morning Yet on Creation Day* (London: Heinemann, 1975), p.16.
6. Qtd. Simon Gikandi, "Chinua Achebe and the Post-Colonial Esthetic: Writing, Identity and the National Formation," *Studies in Twentieth Century Literature*, 15:1 (Winter 1991), p. 32.
7. G.D. Killam, *An Introduction to the Writings of Ngugi* (London: Heinemann, 1980), p.10.
8. Terry Eagleton advocates in *Marxism and Literary Criticism* that literature is an industry controlled by capitalist bourgeoisie. He claims that "books are . . . commodities produced by publishers and sold on the market at a profit.

Drama . . . is a capitalist business which employs certain men (authors, directors, actors, stagehands) to produce a commodity to be consumed by an audience at a profit. Critics are . . . academics hired by the state to prepare students ideologically for their functions within capitalist society. Writers are . . . workers hired by publishing houses to produce commodities which will sell." See also Karl Marx's "Theories of Surplus" which demonstrates how the writers enrich the publishers.

9. ACLALS, 6:1 (Nov. 1982), pp. 76-77.
10. Coleridge's Albatross in "The Rime of the Ancient Mariner" is used metaphorically to depict the effects of colonialism on the colonized. The writers, like the Mariner, have the burden of telling the story.
11. The task of rebuilding an underdeveloped world is likened to the rebuilding situation in the book of Nehemiah. Excavation of the rubbish is essential before foundation laying and structure building: "And Judah said, 'The strength of the bearers of burdens is decayed, and there is much rubbish; so that we are not able to build the wall.'" (4:10)
12. Mali in *Vendor of Sweets* escapes to the US, Obi in *No Longer at Ease* goes to England, G, the narrator of *In the Castle of My Skin,* leaves for Trinidad, and in *The Lonely Londoners,* many Third World immigrants converge in London. Eugene V. Mohr indicates that "London is where West Indian writers go to be published, to be read, to have their reputations established. And in their books London is where people go to become professionals, to enjoy art and culture, to learn the limits of possibility." (33-34) George Lamming suggests that "the men had to leave if they were going to function as writers since books, in that particular colonial conception of literature, were not—meaning, too, are not supposed to be—written by natives." (*The Pleasures* 27) Viney Kirpal's *The Third World Novel of Expatriation: A Study of Emigre Fiction by Indian, West African and Caribbean Writers* is probably the most profound analysis of Third World's escape and escapism through migration.
13. V.S. Naipaul, *Miguel Street* (London: Heinemann, 1974), p. xii.
14. Rotimi Johnson, "The Committed African Writer as Witness and Participant," *South Asian Review of English*, 12-13 (June-Dec. 1986), pp. 130-31
15. Claire L. Dehon, "Africa: Literature and Politics: An Introduction," *STCL* (Writer 1991), p. 7.
16.. Hans M. Zell provides a useful study on the current publishing situation in Africa. He examines and describes the present publishing conditions of several African countries—Nigeria, Kenya, Zambia, Ghana, Sierra Leone, Ivory Coast, Mali, Senegal, Gambia, Zaire, Uganda, Ethiopia, Zimbabwe, South Africa, etc. Zell illustrates the overall publishing situation in Africa in the following manner: "But whereas African publishing may well be booming, so are the problems! Publishing in Africa must be seen as interpreted against a background of many social and infrastructural elements, a diversity of languages, a low rate of literacy, and insufficient number of effective retail outlets, frequently high customs tariffs on

essential manufacturing equipment, severe balance of payments problems in most African countries, and other obstacles, some of near impossible dimensions . . . few African governments attach much significance to their indigenous book industries." (169)

17. Edward W. Said, "Figures, Configurations, Transfigurations," in Anna Rutherford, ed., *From Commonwealth to Post-Colonial* (Sydney: Dangaroo Press, 1992), p. 3.

18. On this point, Peter Nazareth illustrates two main categories; commitment and non-commitment. Nazareth expands this point to indicate how this debate adds another of dimension pressure on Third World writers. To be committed or not, that is the question. After demonstrating his experience of moving from a position of a universal approach to literature to a deeper and more involved approach to literature, especially colonized literature, Nazareth finds himself asking, "Can the African writer in a period of colonialism, nationalism and post-colonialism remain uncommitted? If so, is it desirable that he should remain uncommitted?" (*An African View of Literature* [Evanston: Northwestern Univ. Press, 1974] 1-2) Nazareth admits that the "problem is a complex one, as complex as the problems of colonial and ex-colonial countries." (2) Therefore, colonized writers cannot divorce themselves from the social and political burden of writing committed works.

By commitment, Nazareth means committed to socialism. He points out that "most African writers who condemned colonialism will find themselves committed to socialism. This commitment may be explicit or implicit, as it has been with several writers of other countries." (4) According to the critical standards of a committed work, Ngugi, Soyinka, Anand, Lamming, and La Guma are committed writers, but Achebe, Narayan, Naipaul, and Walcott are not. However, even the uncommitted writers demonstrate sporadic commitment, and they also participate in the process of decolonization in their own ways. For example, Narayan "writes with great insight and sympathy about the 'ordinary' people we might ignore in real life," (Nazareth 160) while Naipaul's biting satire of postcolonial corruption in *The Mimic Men* becomes a prophetic insight of the Caribbean.

19. Qtd. R.S. Morkhandikar, "Commonwealth and Commonwealth Literature: Conceptual Ambiguities," in G.S. Amur et al, *Indian Readings in Commonwealth Literature* (New Delhi: Sterling, 1985), p. 21.

20. Viney Kirpal points out that the Third World writer is a "teacher" and a "voice of his society." The writer, she claims, seeks to educate both the oppressor and the oppressed about the oppressed's living conditions. (5-7)

21 J. Steven Rubin, Interview of Camara Laye, *Africa Report* (Washington: Africana, 1972), p. 22.

22. Qtd. Per Wastberg, ed., *The Writer in Modern Africa* (Uppsala: The Scandinavian Institute of African Studies, 1968), p. 31.

23. Mulk Raj Anand, "Reflections of a Novelist: Some Notes on the Novel," in Amur, p. 8.
24. K.R. Shirwadkar, "Third World Consciousness: Faith and Frustration," in Amur, p. 45.
25. V.S. Naipaul, *The Middle Passage* (New York: Penguin, 1962), p. 29.
26. O.P. Bhatnagar, "Commonwealth Literature: Genesis and Bearings," in Amur, p. 31.
27. Phanuel Akubueze Egejuru, *Towards African Literary Independence: A Dialogue with Contemporary African Writers* (London: Greenwood Press, 1980), p. 4.
28. Qtd. David Cook and Michael Okenimkpe, *Ngugi wa Thiong'o: An Exploration of His Writings* (London: Heinemann, 1983), p. 218.
29. James Ngugi, "Satire in Nigeria," in Pieterse, p. 69.
30. Eldred Durosimi Jones, *The Writing of Wole Soyinka* (Portsmouth, NH: Heinemann, 1988), p. 47.
31. C. Paul Verghese, *Problems of the Indian Creative Writer in English* (Bombay: Somaiya, 1971), p. 133.
32. V.S. Naipaul, *India: A Wounded Civilization* (London: Andre Deutsch, 1976), pp. 31-51.
33. Africans were captured and brought to the West Indies to solve the labour problem. The first batch of slaves arrived in the West Indies in 1672, and thereafter a steady flow of slaves were brought to the Caribbean through the "middle passage." In 1833 slavery was abolished, and in 1838 slaves were emancipated in the Caribbean. These freed slaves abandoned the sugar estates in search of independent livelihood to better their conditions. This situation created a labour shortage. (Hassan 3)
34. To solve the labour problem alluded to in note 33, the colonizers "recruited and indentured" Portuguese and Chinese. These failed to cope with labour conditions, so by foul means Indians were indentured to solve the problem. The Indians proved successful farmers, and they were further enticed or trapped to remain in the Caribbean. According to Hassan, "Indian immigration, which started in 1838 in Guyana and 1845 in Trinidad, punctuated by intermittent breaks, was banned in 1917 because of strong criticisms from Mahatma Gandhi and other Indian leaders." (3-4)
35. Europeans, the colonizers, "established a white obligarch with unlimited political and economic power over the rest of the population." (Hassan 3) Edgar Mittleholzer's works depict this crucial period of the Caribbean history.
36. Dolly Zulakha Hassan, *V.S. Naipaul and the West Indies* (New York: Peter Lang, 1989), p.4.
37. V.S. Naipaul, *A Bend in the River* (New York: Penguin, 1980), p. 3.
38. Robert D. Hammer, "Aspects of National Character: V.S. Naipaul and Derek Walcott," in Satendra Nandan, ed., *Language and Literature in Multicultural Contexts* (Suva, Fiji: University of South Pacific, 1983), p. 179.
39. The term colonial criticism is borrowed from Achebe's "Colonialist Criticism," and it is similar in meaning.

40. Gay Wilentz, "English is a Foreign Anguish: Caribbean Writers and the Disruption of the Colonial Canon," *Decolonizing Tradition: New Views of Twentieth-Century 'British' Literary Canons*, ed. Karen R. Lawrence (Urbana: Univ. of Illinois Press, 1992), p. 261.
41. Janet Batsleer et al, *Rewriting English: Cultural Politics of Gender and Class* (London: Methuen, 1985), pp. 29-30.
42. Qtd. John F. Bayliss, "Ghettoization and Black Literature," in Lloyd W. Brown, ed., *The Black Writer in Africa and the Americas* (Los Angeles: Hennessey and Ingalls, 1973), pp. 81-82.
43. Nick Aaron Ford, "Black Literature and the Problem of Evaluation," in Brown, pp. 61-62.
44. Caribbean literature is the youngest in the context of India and Africa.
45. Jeannette B. Allis, " West Indian Literature: A Case for Regional Criticism," in Roberta Knowles and Erika Smilowitz, ed., *Critical Approaches to West Indian Literature* (St. Thomas, US Virgin Islands: College of the Virgin Islands and UWI, 1981), p. 23.
46. Qtd. James Ngugi, *Homecoming: Essays on African and Caribbean Literature, Culture and Politics* (London: Heinemann, 1972), pp. xviii-xix.
47. Kirpal Singh, "Writers in Limbo: The Third World Experience," *The Literary Criterion*, 23: 4 (1988), pp. 70 and 72.
48. M.J. Fenwick, Introduction, *Writers of the Caribbean and Central America: A Bibliography* (New York: Garland, 1992), vol. I, p. xiii.
49. Narsu K. Nihalani, "English in Third Wrold: Changing Attitudes," in Amur, p. 38.
50. Carolyn Cooper, "Marxist Critical Theory and West Indian Literature: Something Torn and New," in Knowles, p. 47.
51. Kenneth Ramchand, "West Indian Literary History: Literariness, Orality and Periodization," *Callaloo*, 34:2 (1990), p. 96.
52. Information provided by the International Exchange Department of Citibank for September-October 1994.
53. In November 1994, as I made preparation for my Fall 1995 graduate course in Caribbean literature, I discovered that a number of works by Caribbean writers are out of print.
54. Arthur Pollard, "The English Reader and the Commonwealth Writer," *The Commonwealth Review*, 1:1 (1989), p. 35.
55. Eric Sellin, "Reflections on Linguistic and Literary Colonialization and Decolonization in Africa," *STCL*, 15:1 (Winter 1991), pp. 47-48.
56. Similar punishment was meted out to Caribbean students who failed to acquire competency in British English. Several Caribbean writers, including Lamming, Anthony, Naipaul, and Carew, have treated this and other educational themes in their portrayal of a dehumanizing colonial education system.
57. Kitia Touré, writer and filmmaker from Cote d'Ivoire, West Africa, visited Indiana University of Pennsylvania in September 27-October 6, 1993. I am grateful to Kitia and Indiana University of Pennsylvania for such a rich experience of seeing "Africa through an African's eyes," for this first hand

account is representative of Third World writers' situation.

58. Chinua Achebe, "The African Writer and the English Language," in *Morning*, p. 57.
59. Joyce Jonas, *Anancy in the Great House: Ways of Reading West Indian Fiction* (New York: Greenwood Press, 1990), p. 7.
60. George Lamming, *The Pleasures of Exile* (Ann Arbor: Univ. of Michigan Press, 1992), p. 44.
61. Sandra Pouchet Paquet, Foreword to Lamming, *Pleasures*, p. x.
62. Wilson Harris, "The Fabric of the Imagination," in Rutherford, p. 19.
63. Over a decade ago the Caribbean embarked on a plan to gradually replace London exams with Caribbean exams. However, presently students continue to write both GCE and CXC exams.
64. Jean D'Costa, "The West Indian Novelist and Lanugage: A Search for a Literary Medium," *Studies in Caribbean Language*, ed. Alice Carrington (St. Augustine, Trinidad: Univ. of West Indies Press, 1983), p. 252.
65. For example, Guyana was occupied by the Dutch in 1580, but "in the seventeenth and eighteenth centuries, British, French, and Dutch sporadically fought for control over the territory, which changed hands several times before the British finally prevailed in 1803 and thereafter held undisputed occupation and control until Guyana's Independence." (Hassan 2) Guyana obtained independence in 1966.
66. *Selected Poems* (New York: Farrar, 1964), p. 4.
67. Ismith Khan, "Dialect in West Indian Literature," in Brown, p. 149.
68. Jean D'Costa, "Expression and Communication: Literary Challenges to the Caribbean Polydialectal Writers," *The Journal of Commonwealth Literature*, 19:1 (1984), p. 124.
69. S.V. Srinivas, "Politicizing Language: The Relevance of Ngugi's Rejection of English," *Indian Response to African Writing*, ed. A. Ramakrishna Rao and C.R. Visweswara Rao (New Delhi: Prestige, 1993), p. 98.
70. Jemie Onwuchekwa Chinweizu and Madubuike Ihechukwu, *Toward the Decolonization of African Literature* (Washington: Howard Univ. Press, 1983), p. 263.

The Commonwealth Writer and His Obligation: A Study of Indian and African Fiction

A.K. SINHA

Literature is a prism through which the artist projects the various aspects of the social structure in terms of the fictional characters. It is something more than a mere mirror journeying down the high road because the artist is not merely concerned with depicting the social world in largely descriptive terms. The task of the artist is to set his characters in motion within the artificially contrived situations in such a way that they discover values and meanings in the social world. Literature therefore reflects norms, attitudes and values in the sense of the artist's own intention. And a proper study of literature should try to unravel the core of meaning which one finds embedded in the various works of the artists.

Broadly speaking, the commonwealth writer has to expand the consciousness of his people and to retrieve the lost glory of his country. Commonwealth literature generally deals with the literature of the countries once ruled or colonized by the British and thus the socio-economic influence of colonialism on the being of the human beings becomes a common theme with which the writer has to grapple in his own subtly telling way.

Critics of Commonwealth literature have made a distinction between the two movements in colonization: the colonization of people and the colonization of land, producing two different responses. In Australia, Canada and New Zealand the land was colonized for settlement while in India, the West Indies and West Africa the people were colonized and the colonizers had to beat retreats after exploitation and enslavement were no more acceptable.

The purpose of this paper is to link some writers from Africa and India in the aesthetic sense and discover how far one could formulate a framework in which such writers could be viewed collectively. For this, an attempt will be made to look into the metaphysical, social, economic and political commitments of these Commonwealth writers and discuss briefly what are the obligations that they have.

Generally speaking, the people of Africa and India have shared the same colonial crisis of sharp confrontations between east and west in a similar historico-political context. This has been aptly brought out by the Kenyan poet Amin Kassam in his poem "Leper":

You now have
your own farm, mother,
wrestled from hyenas
slippery with the blood
of my elder brothers . . .

yet your hands are soft
you let your cousins
farm your land
and corrupt your sons . . .

While in a corner
I, black sheep,
because of my pigment
stand torn with pain
a leper without a mother.[1]

These lines powerfully sum up the common problem faced by the writer in Africa as well as in India. For, in both cases the writer has to seek solutions to the numerous problems let loose in the native soil because of the colonial past. The blood of the "elder brothers" has been shed to make Africa and India gain freedom from the colonizers. Now the writer has to rebuild the consciousness of his people in the light of the modern developments. So the obligation of the Commonwealth writer is to find in the aspirations of his society new ways of seeking understanding in the light of traditional values as they are confronted with the impact of modern ideas. Rabindranath Tagore voiced a similar sentiment when he wrote in his "Gitanjali" that he wanted his country to awake into that heaven of freedom where the mind was without fear and the head was held high.

The Commonwealth writer in Africa and India has a challenge to face, and the heaven of freedom has to be given a concrete shape by breaking through the narrow domestic walls and by aiming at imparting knowledge which is free. The dignity which the colonized people all but lost during the foreigner's rule has to be regained. The obligation of the Commonwealth writer in Africa and in India is to help their people regain their dignity by showing them in human terms what happened to them, what and how and why they lost their self-esteem. And to make this exposition possible, the Commonwealth writer has to recreate the past and set the scene which is authentic and genuine.

One of the most distressing ills which afflicts the "new nations" is the confusion of values as though they are fixed and eternal—the monopoly of the Western civilization. Although things have changed in the circumambient universe in most of these nations, the hang over of the traumatic experience and effects of their confrontation with Europe seem to still cast their abiding influence on the human consciousness. The Commonwealth writer has to help his society regain belief in itself and put away the complexes of the years of denigration and self-abasement generated during the colonial rule. The writer has to re-educate and regenerate as he is perhaps the most sensitive part of his community.

The Commonwealth writer has to formulate a new set of values, a new frame of reference. He has to bring out the human tragedy, the crisis in the soul of his people. The traditional society in the ancient past in Africa and in India had a healthy balance between the material and the spiritual. Today the materialism has been retained but the spiritual control seems to have disappeared. Swindling and corruption appear to have now become common practices. The village code of conduct has been violated, but a more embracing and bigger code of conduct has not been formulated.

The Commonwealth writer today in Africa and in India has to think of all these things and bring them out in a dramatic and memorable form. He has to think far beyond the imperialist pipe-dreams and the hair-brained chatter of irresponsible frivolity that he might notice in his society. Let us analyze here briefly three West African novelists Ayi Kwei Armah, Chinua Achebe, Mongo Beti and three Indian writers Mulk Raj Anand, R.K. Narayan and Manohar Malgonkar and try to find out whether they could be viewed collectively in a common framework.

The Ghanain novelist Ayi Kwei Armah in his novel *The Beautyful Ones Are Not Yet Born* (1968) has an unnamed hero "the man" who is a worker on the railways, born and brought up in the town with no rural roots to escape to. The deliberate misspelling in the title is to draw the attention of the readers towards the fact that the man, who has not been able to reach heights in spite of his "schooling," represents the semi-educated masses. The man is obsessed with the theme of corruption (which is symbolically presented by the horrifying filth in the social setting). The man tries to retain his honesty and basic simplicity by refusing the bribe offered by Amankwa the "great" timber merchant and contractor. But the man finds that all around him the whole world seems to never tire of saying that there are only two types of men who take refuge in honesty—the cowards and the fools.

This external and internal corruption that the protagonist of this novel finds himself challenged by are neatly juxtaposed against a yawning chasm between the blacks and the white people in Ghana:

> There was no way out visible to us, and out on the hills the white man's gleaming bungalows were so far away, so unreachably far that people did not even think of them in their suffering. And for those who did, there were tales of white men with huge dogs that ate more meat in a single day than a human Gold Coast family got in a month.[2]

This novel of Ayi Kwei Armah reminds one of Mulk Raj Anand's *Coolie* (1936). Munoo, the unlettered boy from the hills is Babu Nathoo Ram's servant who has taken his identity for granted. Like the man in *The Beautyful Ones Are Not Yet Born,* Munoo is a symbol of complete honesty and basic simplicity. It does not occur to him to ask himself what he is apart from being a servant. He finds the people all around him to be superior, but he does not know what constitutes their superiority. Utterly simple that he is, Munoo is thoroughly convinced of his inferiority and he accepts his position as a slave and tries to instill into his mind the notion of his brutishness that his mistress has often nagged him about. He solemnly promises to himself that he would be a good servant, a perfect model of a servant.

There is an underlying pathos in this self-assessment of Munoo, The inferiority complex that has become a basic ingredient of his character is only a result of the repression that has been subtly exercised on him by the society. Munoo becomes a symbol of the oppressed, the downtrodden and the deprived and Babu Nathoo Ram puts across the image of the leisured rich thriving on the colonial system and Mr. England does not know who Munoo is, and according to Mr. Horne all these natives are supposed to be disease-ridden. From the number of lepers in the street he seems to be right for Mr. England. This is the yawning depth of difference between the whites and the "natives." Does not this remind us of the yawning chasm between the blacks and the white people presented in Ayi Kwei Armah's *The Beautyful Ones Are Not Yet Born*?

Chinua Achebe's first novel *Things Fall Apart* (1958) takes the reader to the richly African setting of the traditional Iboland village in Nigeria, where the things are really falling apart and the centre cannot hold. The

Nigerian setting had earlier been caught by the British writer Joyce Cary in his novels entitled *The African Witch* (1951), *Aissa Saved* (1952), *An American Visitor* (1952) and *Mister Johnson* (1952). But these novels of Joyce Cary were primarily concerned with putting together the varied experiences of the writer in a long string of remote colonial posts in the West African bush country. And although these novels gave us interesting accounts of the superstitions and intrigues of the Nigerian village community, they failed to convey an authentic projection of the hopes, fear and aspirations of the African people.

Chinua Achebe with the help of his typically African characters in a genuinely African background, builds up a passionately convincing description of all the repercussions created by the White invaders bringing a new God, a new wealth and new ways in the rural setting. The clash between the African tradition and the white man's "modernity" is presented by the author with a mildly comic irony:

> The white man had indeed brought a lunatic religion, but he had also built a trading store and for the first time palm-oil and kernel became things of great price, and much money flowed into Umuofia.
>
> And even in the matter of religion there was a growing feeling that there might be something in it after all, something vaguely akin to method in the overwhelming madness.
>
> This growing feeling was due to Mr. Brown, the white missionary, who was very firm in restraining his flock from provoking the wrath of the clan. . . . One of the great men in the village was called Akunna and he had given one of his sons to be taught the white man's knowledge in Mr. Brown's school.[3]

The progression in the taking over of Umuofia by the Whites seems to be completed. This description reminds one of the following disclosure made by R.K. Narayan:

> When I was five years old I was initiated into the mysteries of letters with the appropriate religious ceremonials. I was taught to shape the first two letters of the alphabet on corn spread out on a tray, both in Sanskrit and Tamil. Sanskrit, because it was the classical language of India, Tamil because it was the language of the province in which I was born and my mother tongue. But in the classroom neither of these two languages was given any importance; they were assigned to the most helpless among the teachers, the pundits who were treated as a joke by the boys, since they

> taught only the 'second language,' the first being English as ordained by Lord Macaulay when he introduced English education in India.[4]

Does not this school to which the child R.K. Narayan has been sent remind one of Mr. Brown's school referred to by Chinua Achebe where the white man's knowledge is being taught? Do not Chinua Achebe and R.K. Narayan share a common note of protest against the "white man's burden"?

Let us take just one more illustration from the Cameroonian author Mongo Beti's novel entitled *Mission to Kala* (1958) in which the anti-heroic observer-narrator-protagonist Medza is told by Bikokolo:

> Shall I tell you what your special thunder is? Your certificates, your learning, your knowledge of white man's secrets. Have you any idea what these up-country bushmen will quite seriously believe about you? That you only have to write a letter in French, or speak French to the nearest District Officer, to have anyone you like imprisoned, or get any personal favour you want. That's the kind of idiocy you'll find waiting for you.[5]

The reader knows that Medza has failed his examinations. And so when his cousin Zambo introduces Medza to the village people in Kala as one who has won every diploma they can think of and as one who sits on the same benches as the sons of white men, dramatic irony is generated. Underneath this somewhat comic strain can be noticed an underlying note of seriousness. For the people in Kala, Medza is the white man, and the hunger for knowing the mysteries of the whites shows how deep the effects of colonialism have become. Learning the foreign language and going to school have become the prized possessions for which the villagers pine.

There seems to be a faulty planning which is basically responsible for this chaos in human thinking. The black children in the schools are being taught the ancestral wisdom of the whites. Matters would certainly have been different if these children were taught their own ancestral wisdom.

Krishnan, the protagonist of R.K. Narayan's *The English Teacher* (1946) expresses a similar point of view when he affirms:

> My mind was made up. . . . At first I had thought of sending in my resignation by letter to Brown, and making an end of it. . . . I would send in a letter which would be a classic in its own way, and

> which would singe the fingers of whoever touched it. In it I was going to attack a whole century of false education. I was going to explain why I could no longer stuff Shakespeare and Elizabethan metre and Romantic poetry for the hundredth time into young minds and feed them on the dead mutton of literary analysis and theories and histories, while what they needed was lessons in the fullest use of the mind. This education had reduced us to a nation of morons: we were strangers to our own cultures and camp followers of another culture feeding on leavings and garbage. (205)

Though Krishnan later reacts against this idea as a rabid attack on all English writers and feels that there is something far deeper that he wishes to say, the point is actually made.

The young minds, according to Achebe, Beti and Narayan have been given the education of the colonial system, and have been asked to grow with two fathers pulling them in opposite directions. The father at home and the father at the school have been consistently pulling the young in two directions and the over-all effect of these pulls and pressures has weighed so heavily on the well being of the people concerned.

Manohar Malgonkar's *Open Season* (1978) is a novel which subtly projects the various nuances of the cross-cultural contacts which take place when young people of India and America change their places and try to adjust in their new surroundings. The novel presents Jaikumar (Jake), Krishnaswamy (Sammy) and Neela Rawat as the young Indians trying to find their new bearings in the distant land. Mr. Sabnis talks about his son Krishnaswamy to Jaikumar and Mr. Rachappa: Remember he will be a big man when he comes. . . . An America-trained engineer. Someone with a brilliant future. Tatas and Birlas will come competing for his services and prospective fathers-in-law with fat dowries." (7-8)

A similar theme is dealt with by Ayi Kwei Armah in his novel *Fragments* (1969) which emerges from the following dialogue between Efua and Juana:

> "Tell me!" the woman said, "what is there that so many of our young people go there and do not want to return? I am not the only one."
>
> "I don't know," Juana answered. "You think it is something there holding him?
>
> "What else could it be?"
>
> "Things here he is afraid of coming back to?" (51)

Thus it is evident that all these Commonwealth writers share a common obligation to their society. Ayi Kwei Armah, Mulk Raj Anand, Chinua Achebe, R.K. Narayan, Mongo Beti and Manohar Malgonkar may be writing from different points of the globe. But the social, economic and political problems which they are grappling with in their own ways are so similar that these writers can be easily studied as different shades of the same spectrum. They share a common metaphysical concern for the shadows cast on the growing minds of their people by the hydrahead of colonialism. Their people, according to these authors, appear to be like men left to their own devices in a world which did not belong to them, and which they had not made and did not understand. These writers are one in the aesthetic sense. They successfully project the trials and tribulations of the consciousness of their people through their authentically realized characters presented in a genuinely authentic setting. It is the precarious relation to the white world that unites all these writers. It is the necessity to remake the world in their own image that can be called the common concern and the common obligation of these Commonwealth writers.

NOTES

1. *African Voices*, ed. Howard Sergeant (London: Evans Brothers, 1973).
2. Ayi Kwei Armah, *The Beautyful Ones Are Not Yet Born* (African Writers Series, 1969), pp. 77-78.
3. Chinua Achebe, *Things Fall Apart* (African Writers Series, 1977), pp. 161-62.
4. M.K. Naik, *Aspects of Indian Writing in English* (Macmillan India, 1979), p. 19.
5. Mongo Beti, *Mission to Kala* (African Writers Series, 1964), p. 15.

Postcolonial Attitude towards the Teaching of English Poetry in the Commonwealth Countries with Special Reference to India

RAJITA SAI BABA

This paper is devoted to a discussion of the aims and objectives of teaching English literature in the native and non-native situations. It also considers the role of sensibility, in the teaching of English literature in the postcolonial Commonwealth countries. The student's knowledge of tradition, value *foci* and religious and social values, acquired by him through 'non-formal' means, also influence his sensibility. This kind of acquisition of tradition is possible in India due to a sense of belonging to society and the uniquely unbroken nature of tradition. Hence, the pressure it exerts on the student is instinctive and yet not rudimentary. Thus, the frame of reference, even when it lacks 'formality' is vital enough in its connected comprehensiveness and, perhaps, more important than formal training in the mother tongue literature. Placing English literature in such a frame acquires an importance and dynamism and is easily identifiable by anyone sufficiently and seriously involved in the teaching of English literature in India. An attempt has been made to explore some possibilities of making use of the student's knowledge of his mother tongue literature in teaching English literature.

The traditional opinion is that literature is taught for ethical, moral and cultural purposes. Matthew Arnold, in his dispute with T.H. Huxley, and F.R. Leavis with C.P. Snow, strongly claimed that the primary aim of teaching literature is cultural transference. Leavis feels that an intelligent reading of literature "trains a sense of value." James Reeves, who belongs to the Leavisian school of thought, says that "no nation" which claims to give its citizens a full cultural education can neglect its poetry. L.C. Knights feels that the readers of literature find the meaning of something they have been trying to find "with a spurt of intellectual energy that does not dissipate itself in momentary pleasure." It makes the reader capable of making connections with other works of literature and with experience as a whole. He thinks that the duty of a teacher of literature is to help the student experience "the spurt of intellectual energy" and "make necessary connections." F.R. Leavis and L.C. Knights represent the traditional cultural-ethical aim of teaching literature with varying emphases.

William Evans and Jerry Walker Represent the new method Whose objectives are very different from those of cultural-ethical school discussed above. They say: "The time poetry was taught mainly for its sociological and historical value is past. It is become less common to find literature, still selected, organized and taught, primarily as a means of gaining insight into life and its problems. Today literature is taught chiefly as a means of gaining insight into literature itself." Evans and Walker feel that each work of poetry has its own structure and its own combination of elements. The teacher's duty, according to them, is to help students recognize the structure of a given work of poetry. The classroom strategy will be to take a large number of selections and arrive through them generalities with the help of similar sets of questions about poems and value. Thus, according to the new method, the only aim of studying poetry, perhaps, is to gain insight into the formal features of the poem itself. As a part of the overhauling of the American education system, consequent to Russia's launching of the Sputnik, the new method is said to be effectively used in the united States. In the recent decades the centre of emphasis in teaching poetry, more or less, has shifted from the content to the form. But a comprehensive teaching method of poetry will, most probably, include both the content and the form as neither of them can exist in isolation.

The opinions discussed so far in this paper consider only the first language situation of teaching poetry, and, in a way, do not visualize the various constraints of teaching content and form in a non-native situation. English syllabi are largely adapted from the British universities and the aims and objectives of teaching a heavily literature-based English syllabi have never been clearly defined. Though the Sadler Commission of the Calcutta University (1917) was very critical about it, this problem failed to attract the attention of the authorities concerned until 1971. The Study Group (English) which went into the problem of defining the objectives of teaching English poetry in India states them as follows: "The ability to read the prescribed standard literary classics and related reference works, so as to: (a) Grasp the meaning of words in literary contexts, (b) draw inferences from what is read, (c) understand and evaluate the ideas expressed in the passages read, (d) recognize and analyze metaphor, imagery, and syntactic and other literary devices, and

(e) distinguish different literary pieces and styles of writing." However, a suitable methodology and syllabus to achieve these objectives were not suggested by the Study Group. The syllabus suggested, in a way, continues to be in the old tradition and cannot easily be taught in a foreign language situation. The university departments of English and other syllabus-framing bodies also do not appear to have made serious attempts to restructure the syllabi to achieve the objectives set by the Study Group.

Holloway argues that English poetry should be taught to acquaint the students in Afro-Asian countries with the history, culture and the modes of thinking of Britain. The same author, speaking specifically about teaching English poetry in India, says that "it should be an important part of at least the better sub-continent student's work in English literature, that it should lead him forward to some general notion of the basic factors in English civilization at various times in the past." The arguments of Holloway, in spite of their being lofty, are not applicable to a non-English, independent country like India. English in the present context is not the language of the colonial masters. It is the language of communication within the Commonwealth nations and a window on the knowledge of the world for the Indian intellectual. Hence, English can be used to understand the world culture in its variety and totality rather than only as a tool to know "the English civilization at various times in the past." To attain this goal "English literature" may have to be redefined as "Literature in English." It is the sum total of the translations available in English from all the world literatures and the original writings in English done by the native and non-native writers of English. A change in the definition of the subject may, perhaps, bring about a change in the objective of teaching it. "Literature in English" rather than "English Literature" will probably be a more effective tool in achieving the objective of cross-cultural fertilization through cross-cultural understanding.

Ronald Bottrall feels that the non-native students fail to comprehend what they think "exotic" in English literature. He shows how William Wordsworth's "Resolution and Independence" fails to communicate if students cannot visualize a leech-gatherer. It is not because our culture is inferior but it is an altogether different culture. The literary tastes of different nationalities and culture-groups show considerable divergence. The differences in socio-cultural background result in difference in the framework of literary taste. In India the romantic and the philosophical schools of poetry make a deep impression.

An awareness of the difference in the dynamics of literary tastes of different nationalities and culture-groups and the general inability to respond fully to a culturally alien work of poetry may perhaps lead to the question, "from what background does a student respond to a work of poetry in a foreign language?" Poetic sensibility can be defined as one single and indivisible faculty of responding to a poem. The process of its formation is both conscious and unconscious. It is organized into a system, most probably by the first literature the student comes into contact with, which, in most cases, will be the mother tongue literature. Hence, it can be suggested that a student's response to a work of literature in a foreign language is against the background of his unconsciously inhered sensibility and consciously acquired knowledge of his mother tongue literature. A student may understand a poem in a foreign language better in comparison or contrast with the two aspects of his native poetic sensibility.

In the context of teaching English poetry in India the problem of native sensibility has some important pedagogical implications. It explains why some English authors are more acceptable to the Indian students than the others. This awareness is academically significant because it influences the principles underlying the selection of text books and their teachability. Simplifying somewhat, one might say that an English writer may appeal to an Indian student if: (a) he is more universal and less culture-bound, (b) he touches his native poetic sensibility, (c) his works relate meaningfully with a body of mother tongue literature the student is already familiar with, (d) he has influenced the mother tongue literature of the students with which the student is fairly familiar before he comes to the study of English literature. Very often the appeal of a work of literature to a culture outsider depends upon more than one of these factors. Though it is almost impossible to determine why a culture outsider like the Indian student responds favourably to a work of English poetry, an attempt can be made to analyze his responses. As there are no verifiable data, this attempt cannot avoid being speculative.

Shakespeare's appeal is universal in spite of the fact that he is the best example of Elizabethanism. Shakespeare's sense of poetic justice, the pattern of Good and Evil in his works have an unmistakable appeal to Indian sensibility. Shakespeare's poetry in certain aspects resembles poetry of Kalidasa and Bhasa. Milton's epics, especially *Paradise Lost* and the Indian puranic tradition have several meeting points in content and form. The grand allusive style that Milton uses in his epic poems is a common phenomenon in all Indian literatures. As K. Subrahmanian feels, Indians have a penchant for the florid and look for a similar rhetoric in a foreign language also.

Wordsworth, Shelley and Keats were the main inspirations for the romantic movements in almost all Indian poems in the first and the second decades of this century. Wordsworth appeals to the Indian sense of the mystical with his preoccupation with pantheism and rebirth which are matters of deep conviction in India. Shelley, with his spirit of revolt and reform, attracted the attention of the Indian intellectuals and poets who were greatly dissatisfied with the British colonial exploitation and the frozen Indian social structure. A group of romantice poets and the early progressive poets in Telugu have been influenced by Shelley's philosophy of life and poetry. Keats, like the Indian philosophers, believes that suffering is the essence of life and evil a reality. Prabas Jeevan Chowdary feels that Keats found an aesthetic solution to the problems of evil and suffering and that his solution is allied to that of Indian aesthetics.

T.S. Eliot's notion of the purpose of poetry is close to that of Indian aesthetics. Eliot himself says, "I know my poetry shows the influence of Indian thought and sensibility." Hence, an Indian student can be successfully motivated to study his poetry. Eliot's allusive poetic style is, perhaps, not very strange to a Telugu student because it has some common features with the "Prabandha" style of poetry which was in vogue in the sixteenth and the seventeenth centuries and is still followed by a small number of neo-classical poets. Eliot's *Four Quartets* resembles rather closely the mystic "sataka" poetry in Telugu, though the formal pattern differs. W.B. Yeats's interest in Indian occultism, his idea of love, his great range of poetic experience, his use of folk mythology appeal to Indian sensibility. W.H. Auden, Stephen Spender and C. Day Lewis were the sources of inspiration to the progressive school of poets in Telugu.

Approaching English literature through native sensibility and the mother tongue literature of the student cannot possibly be successful unless the English literatures syllabi are recast with a view to facilitating this approach. The average teacher of English literature will have to acquire a fairly good knowledge of the mother tongue literature and the Indian aesthetic tradition in its classical and folk manifestations. Neither of these requirements can be taken for granted in the present circumstances. The former asks for a change in the outlook of the syllabus-framing bodies and the latter, which is dependent upon the former, is more difficult to achieve. Hence, this approach cannot be a substitute for any of the present approaches and its practical utility, at least for the present, will have to be marginal and supplementary.

Epic is another form of English poetry which can be taught in the same way. An English epic like *Paradise Lost* is a combination of Indian 'Purana' and 'Kavya.' The epic features of *Paradise Lost* can be compared and contrasted with the five features of the purana and the eighteen features of the 'Kavya.' Students may feel a sense of discovery if the teacher could build in some student participation into this activity by setting tasks. Students can be asked to discover the nearest Indian literary form to ballad, ode, lyric etc., and a work of literature in his mother tongue. If time permits, the formal features in both the works can be discussed in comparison and contrast. An awareness of differences in formal features also clarifies the student's understanding of the form of English poem in hand.

Indian dramatic tradition, which is essentially poetic, in some aspects, resembles Shakespeare's art. Paul Edwards says that one of the pleasures of teaching English literature overseas is the occasional discovery that a work of English literature can take new life from the alien environment of the student. This is likely to happen when the student responds to an English poem from his native background and value-patterns and tries to determine its value. Edwards discusses this aspect of response from his experience of teaching Wordsworth's 'Michael' in Africa. The Indian and African value-patterns with regard to the sentiments expressed in the poem are not very different from each other.

'Michael,' which expresses a peasent's feeling for landed property and its inheritance, according to Edwards, is an alien poem in the modern industrial England. But in rural India ceiling of land still remains a painful experience as it was to Michael. Besides, family ties in India, in spite of the recent erosion, are still less loose than what they are now in England. 'Michael' has a special lesson to offer to Indian students, who like the nephew and the son of Michael, want to desert their home villages lured by the attraction of life in the city. If the teacher emphasizes the bond between the peasant and the land, the closeness of family ties and the lure of the city for the present-day youth, 'Michael' may appeal more powerfully to the sensibility of the Indian student than to his British counterpart.

Another class room strategy that may produce some awareness of technique in the student is a comparison of the styles of the poets in both languages. D.V. Krishna Sastri, Vedalu, Arudra, Buchibabu and Sri Sri imitated Shelley, Keats, Eliot, Maugham and Joyce respectively.

Shakespeare's plays, some romantic, Victorian and modern poets, and some fiction has been translated fairly satisfactorily into Telugu. Some teachers feel that a good translation, if sparingly and judiciously used, is likely to enhance the student's experience of the original text. Some others like Dorothy Hayes De Huneeus strongly oppose the use of translation in teaching a foreign literature. She says, "Translation is either of no value or definitely undesirable, a barrier between the student and any possibility he may have of developing a real feeling for English style."

The problem of translation brings into focus the role of languages in the teaching of a foreign literature. The difficulty of understanding the language differs from genre to genre in the context of teaching foreign poetry. In a teaching situation, 'Metaphor' in a poem may not, probably, carry with them an equal importance of language.

This approach, if not used judiciously, is likely to develop in the student simplistic notions of English literature based on his inadequate knowledge of mother tongue literature and a mechanical study of comparisons and contrasts. This may, in turn, prevent the student from responding to English poetry fully and comprehensively. The teacher of English literature will have to make use of this approach carefully so that it helps the students to achieve the connected comprehensiveness mentioned in the introduction to this paper.

English literature syllabi in most of the universities do not take into consideration the problems involved in teaching a text which is emotionally and experientially alien in a non-English country like India. The place of a text in a syllabus is almost always determined by its status in the history of English literature. Hence, English syllabi have to be designed in such a way that they include poets and authors who can be compared and contrasted with their counterparts in the mother tongue literature of the student. This approach may become more feasible if Indian English writing and literature translated from Indian languages also form part of the English literature syllabi.

The next important limitation of this approach is that it takes for granted the ability of the teacher to implement this approach and the readiness of the student to cooperate with the teacher. Few teachers of English literature can be expected to have a good knowledge of the mother tongue poetry and the dynamics of native Indian sensibility. This approach demands both training and skill on the part of the teacher. The problem can be thoroughly or partly solved by introducing a course in the comparative study of literature at the postgraduate level. This course may serve the purpose better if comparative study in the Indian context and the methodology of the comparative study as a pedagogical approach are given equal importance. This approach expects the student to study some movements of literature and authors in his mother tongue literature besides the prescribed poems in English. This involves problems of taste and motivation.

In spite of these limitations the role of the native sensibility and the mother tongue literature in responding to English literature is of vital importance because "it is impossible to conceive of a person standing beyond his culture. His culture has brought him into being in every respect, has given his categories and habits of thought, his range of feeling, his idiom and tones of speech."

Indian Women's Voices: The Postcolonial and Post-Modernist Era

LAKSMISREE BANERJEE

Indian women's literature in English, still a marginalized area of critical study, is slowly gaining ground as a significant and identifiable area of research. The woman writer's reconstruction of life through the various literary forms and modes emphasizes the validity of Beheroze Shroff's statement: "The time has come for women to stop seeing through men's eyes and language—we have to have a different women's voice." The Indian English women writers of the first phase of development wrote during the crucible years of the 1950s and 1960s of nation building and consequent decolonization. This paper will touch upon the post-modern second generation women, writing in the recent past of the 70s, 80s and 90s, closer to and more conversant with real life movements and modern-day complexities, handling the English medium with more grace, effortlessness, ease and a specifically organized abandon. In this modest exploration, dealing primarily with the lyric and short story forms handled by Indian women writers in English, Simone de Beauvoir's assessment of women's literature becomes quite pertinent. "Feminine literature," she says, "is animated less by a wish to demand our rights than by an effort towards clarity and understanding." The enjoyment and interpretation of such literature, hence, can be quite fruitful without having a sexist bias. It is a long time since Simone de Beauvoir published *The Second Sex* (1949) in which her assertion, of a non-sexist and non-prejudiced attitude towards the world of women, established and created a new place for women as equal beings in the existing world order. Her purpose was not so much to reform or transform as to explain the deep-rooted causes for such a bias against women. Women, she said, were assigned a secondary position, not by virtue of natural qualities or biological necessity but by a world controlled by a patriarchal society. In this voyage towards rationalization and understanding it is evident that all the inequities and illogicalities suffered by women earlier have more or less decreased with the passage of time and women have assumed new role models for the benefit of the self and society. Women writers in India have emerged as a distinct group not only because of the valid and authentic literary quality of their compositions but also because such feminine compositions may be considered 'sociolect' whose force, value and power in effecting social change and amelioration cannot be negated.

'Postcolonial' and 'post-modernist,' though not having exactly the same literary or critical implications, are relevant terms in designating the fast and progressive tendencies in women's writings to grow out of the trappings and set patterns of a conventional English idiom, constricting diction and stilted language of the past to a new zone of free, uninhibited and genuinely creative effusions. Such spontaneous outpourings have been competently restructured into literary genres like the lyric and the short story which call for serious intellectual study. The lyric and the short story are essentially brief and graphic forms in which the innate creativity, the persona of the woman writer with regard to her immediate environment and situation, come out laconically in what may be termed organized flashes. In both these forms the Indian English women writers share a common, simple and unpretentious platform from which they imbibe as well as analyze the central core of contemporary Indian realities. They are articulate, transparent as well as deeply conscious of their own identity as women and as writers.

There can be no doubt that the most exciting cultural development in the last few decades of the century is the evolution and steady growth of a standardized bulk of Indian women's literature in English. In this postcolonial and post-modernist era women have outgrown their earlier plagiaristic and assimilative modes, which mainly seemed to be an extension of male literature or established forms of such writings. Indian women, writing in English today, are an urbane, sophisticated and intellectually alert lot with a proper English education; hence they have become more innovative, experimental, confessional and realistic than they were ever before, their creative efforts being largely fresh and experience-based.

There are certain interesting and relevant points under which Indian women's literature in English needs to be studied:

a) As a social document, women being both victims and agents of social change.
b) As a study of the Indian female psyche in its interaction and correlation with the male psyche.
c) As a dialectic arising from the conflict of gender and genre constructions.

d) As a problem of the 'androgynous' element in Indian women's writings.
e) As an analysis of the specific usage of certain myths, image-structures and symbols for the re-definition of womanhood vis-a-vis Indian society.
f) As a case-study of the emerging traditional and non-traditional roles and images of women; of the normative models from ancient to modern times with particular reference to the emergence of the New Woman: the image of the Rebel and Liberator taking precedence over that of the Mother.
g) As a confessional and personal mode used increasingly in the authentic portrayal of the inner and outer life of women in India.
h) As those particular literary and linguistic elements which make women's literature distinctive from that of men.
i) As a study of contemporaneity as well as feminine identity in the post-modernist world.
j) As a study of women's voices which affirm the innermost strength and particularity of women, their literature being more a distinctive part of a genre than generic.

The short story may be described as having evolved from the typically Indian age-old art form of story-telling. Although it is a relatively modern development in terms of its present form, its skilful handling by women writers in more recent times, has lent it a peculiarly feminine charm, intensity and lucidity. It would not be an exaggeration to state that short stories such as "The Farewell Party" by Anita Desai, "Rhythms" by Lakshmi Kannan, "Babuji's Dost" by Indrani Aikath-Gyaltscn and "My Beloved Charioteer" by Shashi Deshpande exude a certain lyrical fluidity and thematic and technical maturity which may be comparable with that of the best short stories of world literature today. The Indian English women writers also display a remarkable skill and aesthetic fluency in handling English as an easy medium of communication and creative expression. A typical paragraph from Anita Desai's "The Farewell Party" reveals the naturalness of the prose, its closeness to real life speech rhythms and the richness and accuracy of detail which helps to create a wonderful vignette of contemporary Indian life in a small town. She writes, "These women she had always encountered in just such a ring as they formed now, the kind that garden babblers form under a hedge where they sit gabbling and whirring with social bitchiness, and she had always stood outside it, smiling stiffly, not wanting to join and refusing their effusively nodded invitation. They were the wives of men who represented various mercantile companies in the town—

and although they might seem exactly alike to one who did not belong to this circle, inside it were subtle gradations of importance according to the particular company for which each one's husband worked and of these only they themselves were initiates."[1] There are several operative phrases such as 'social bitchiness,' 'subtle gradations,' 'this circle' and 'stood outside it' which manifest the objective distancing as well as subjective involvement and empathy with which the woman writer delineates her immediate environment. The simplicity, directness and veracity of the literary text is commendable. Such short stories reveal an impeccable awareness of the varied Indian scenario with regard to the Indian women, of its constant and changing values, of the different types and classes of women and their characters; they also unravel a complex modern sensibility poised against thoughtlessness, obsolescence and insensitivity, the need to conform and to revolt, as well as narrative devices conveying the inevitability of situation, the tempo, the mood, the psychological concern with character and the climactic twist or reversal, all of which contribute to the merit of such writings.

These women writers are deeply aware of the various facets of domestic and public life, of the different aspects of human and social relationships which bring them both happiness and anxiety, physical and spiritual concerns and upheavals which are adequately expressed in the text. There is a definite search for an alternative vision or an artistic transcendence which make these compositions significant and purposeful. In "Jahanara's Tomb," a short story of a faithless and promiscuous husband and a suffering wife, overpowered by the memories of love and tender devotion, Malathi Rao seems to offer solace and a way out of the trauma to the woman protagonist: "There she waited for death to come and release her. Everyday she woke up to peer at the sun beyond. True, the city was out there, vibrant with love, life and laughter. Sometimes the sunrays pricked her eyes through the window . . . then she moved her limbs in remembered pleasure of walks under the green summer trees, felt the soft grass under her feet. What an age ago it all seemed. . . . A monument of chaste white marble was what she sought now—where she could kneel and pray and wash herself clean, in preparation of the last judgement."[2] The entire exercise and experience of marriage is reflected upon as a sin and aberration of the woman in love who, like Jahanara, should have remained single and self-sufficient without succumbing to the perdition of a man's betrayal. More than the Indianization or indigenization of the language and idiom, women writers are concerned today with the quality of experience, the refinement of perception, the transmutative processes of artistic recreation and the intensified presentation of an alternative ideal.

It is important to understand in the study of feminine writings the close relationship between the literary and the social structures of consciousness which are often overlapping, as much as the analogy and contrast between the woman writer, her problems, attitudes and spheres of expression vis-a-vis those of the male writer and his area of writing. What women writers share today is much more than what separates them. While closely examining the various literary genres we are able to foreground such common perspectives and approaches. In doing so we also obtain a clear view of the constant interplay and conflict of the gender and genre constructions, of the typically feminine and the generally human world order and paradigms. The most important aspect of Indian English feminine writing, hence, becomes the vibrant element of controversy which ceaselessly illumines and enriches the narrative or the poetic fabric. These women writers form a distinct literary group not by virtue of their radical or assertive feministic stance but by that of the parallel rhythms of complementariness as well as sex-based singularities evinced in their compositions. The postcolonial era of women's writings does not suffer any more from a colonial tradition of subjection or subversion of a weaker group. The colonial hang over is now a thing of the past both in terms of language and attitude and its theories outmoded and exploded; new forms and post-modernist norms have evolved in which women writers have grown in stature and grown meaningfully into a new intellectual tradition of a living dialogue with artistically relevant and socially specific realities. Indian English women writing is no more esoteric or belligerent but a shared experience; it is what may be designated as a "living utterance,"[3] (with apologies to Mikhail Bakhtin) which unifies the reader and the read, the subject and the object, the woman writer and her audience, the feminine milieu and the world at large.

The most interesting point which arises in the critical study of feminine literature is the use of the term 'androgyny.' As originally borrowed from Coleridge by Virginia Woolf, it described the freedom of the writer, to use, during the process of creative expression, any such concepts or mental acts as may be attributed to either male or female. The androgynous mind 'is resonant and porous; it transmits emotion without impediment: it is naturally creative, incandescent and undivided.'[4] From denoting duality it has come to denote artistic completeness or even the Keatsian perception of 'negative capability' through which the woman writer perceives and portrays characters and situations both identifiably feminine as well as generally human; hence, often the woman's experiences of pleasure or pain become an integral part of the real world of human beings as a species. A perfect example is detectable in the character of Miss Krishna in Nergis Dalal's short story "The Connoisseur." 'Miss Krishna had a nervous, slightly frenetic appearance' with a love for collecting unusual items like 'silver statues, carved figurines, watches, jewellery, monogrammed ice-tongs, egg cups made of polished wood' a trait which may be specified as that of a woman; yet she suffers from kleptomania or the pilfering disease which is common to both male and female. Another such example of an androgynous structure is found in Anita Desai's short story "The Accompanist" in which the relationship between the ustad or maestro and his accompanying tanpura player is described thus: "Ours is a world formed and defined and enclosed not so much by music as by a human relationship on solid ground level—the relationship of love. Not an abstract quality, like music, or an intellectual one, like art, but a common human quality lived on an everyday level of reality. What else is in it that weaves us together. . . . Is this not love? No marriage was closure."[5]

The women's movement as an organized force in the 70s, 80s and 90s with city-based autonomous as well as national women's groups coordinating campaigns and raising their voices against the deprivation and exploitation of women, has resulted in a new and unique post-modernist literature by Indian women. In this kind of English literature we find a wonderful blend of social, political and literary elements in the voice of the woman writer; here the picture of the woman as a helpless victim and the man as a relentlessly dominating master gets transformed to one in which the woman celebrates her struggle and victory against the imbalance and illegitimacy of a male-dominated culture. This difference in the woman's image and text in the postcolonial decades brings about the paradoxical and antithetical contexture of gender and genre, of feminism and androgyny, of tradition and independence in the Indian English women's writings today. The new generation of women writers has emerged from both subjugation and aggressiveness to a state of total equanimity and equality in clear perception of their goals in the future. Now passion, agony and pathos underlie as a strong foundation and refined substructure the primary fabric of aesthetic creation. Hegemonic initiatives have given way to more egalitarian currents in the Indian English women's literature with 'feminism' and 'Indianness' easily blending into the 'natural' and the 'universally human.' The backlash, of extreme conservatism on the one hand and of 'feminism' on the other, has contributed positively to an emergent woman's order most definitely assured of its dignified place in the new world order. As a result Indian women's literature in English stands in its own right, now, as internationally and humanistically more tenable. The harsh inequities perceptible in the earlier texts have dissolved into a subtle and mellowed re-creation of values more fundamental to human life in general—'feminism' a dogma, has given way to 'womanism,' a reality and an indisputable necessity for world progress and civilizational change for the better. 'Post-modernism' and 'postcolonialism' in this context is not a movement counter to 'classicism' or 'traditionalism' but one in which both are incorporated towards a new kind of dialectic and dynamism, a new kind of art in which realism and romanticism, technical discipline and vehement effusion interact within a single plane of creative experience.

In terms of literary and aesthetic quality it has been widely acclaimed that women are better writers because they are more faithful to their experience and feelings and also that the feminine principle in nature is directly linked with that of creativity. Says Ashish Nandy in his essay on *Woman versus Womanliness*: "In the twilight zone in which the creative mind dwells, there is always a certain stress upon the ability to turn inwards—the ability to accept intuition and tenderness as values—a certain sensitivity to one's natural environment and to the latent communications among human beings; and the capacity to use self-expression which mobilizes feelings and imageries. In the West this has invariably meant becoming feminine."[6] It is this veracity and sensitivity to one's inner self and immediate environment that enriches the literary text of women writers. While critically examining the body of such literature, the congruity and the variety, the similarity and the individuality among such writers is striking. For example, Sunita Jain's short story "A Dead Wife" is, in some ways, similar to Jai Nimbkar's "The Childless One." In both, the women protagonists have to a large extent sacrificed and persevered in love and in acquiescence to keep their hearth and home running, yet failed in obtaining respect from their male counterparts. While the young, second wife of the old husband in Sunita Jain's story submits to the reality that her husband will not give her children because she was married, in the first place, to look after the children of his dead wife (a strange but normal 'Indian' situation in which the dead takes precedence over the living and obsolete social customs over human feelings) the wife in Nimbkar's story revolts. After being rejected by her husband for having a tumour in her stomach, instead of a child, she goes through the ordeals of life with courage while giving birth to a child from another man. When her husband calumniates her saying "You filthy whore; whose son is he?" she avenges herself saying "He is not yours, that's for sure." This vindication of a woman's standpoint, which is common to most women's writings, is not merely a feminist statement but that of a particular perspective which has to be projected as equally valid and important in the real world of affairs. A special kind of complexity is thus discernible in feminine literature today, a dialectic which arises from "overlapping worlds of experience. . . the world of myth and fantasy and the world of high technology; the world of traditional ritual and a modern, sceptical world; the world of collective responsibilities and the world of the individual. What is of interest is the tension or negotiation between such worlds and the sudden sharp slippage from one into another."[7]

In the postcolonial and post-modernist decades, in the aftermath of war, imperialism and subversion of the weak, with changing political and social conditions, overt feminism and blatant voices of dissent have amalgamated with more universal themes of loneliness, childhood, age, sexuality, death and poverty. Against a generally expansive canvas, the Indian women's question and issues form the core of mainstream women's writings in English. Shashi Deshpande, in "My Beloved Charioteer" shares the same conceptualization of Indian widowhood as that of Indrani Aikath-Gyaltsen in "Colony No. 48."[8] The Indian widow is no longer a symbol of love, sorrow and bereavement—on the contrary she is a strong human being who strives to come out of the shackles of a ruthless and insensitive regime of male domination. The sophisticated lady in Shashi Deshpande's story is as much a victim of terror and suppression as the factory worker's wife in Aikath-Gyaltsen's story; both are relieved with the death of their husbands. In this context Gyaltsen's poem "The Widower" comes easily to mind: marriage, in the post-modern world, is seen as an institution which subjugates the individual, and contrary to the earlier myths, throttles freedom, love, respect and desire for each other. Says Gyaltsen:

> He went into the room where the coffin lay . . . .
> 'I am free now,' said he.
> He had said it many times since
> The moment he suspected his wife's silence,
> Realized that the bitch had died in her sleep
> He left the prospect of freedom unexplored.
> It was less from a feeling of remorse than
> From not knowing what to do with the gift.

Gyaltsen's stories like "Babuji's Dost" and novelette *Daughters of the House* assert, unambiguously and undauntedly, the woman's viewpoint. Her women protagonists have grown in stature from those of the first phase of feminine literature—they are no longer silent rebels but bold, outspoken and action-oriented beings ready to take the most daring decisions to effect reversals for the better. Radhika, in "Babuji's Dost," exonerates herself from 'the limbo' of a four-month-old marriage even though she is neither supported nor accepted by her parents. The father has a 'stern, forbidding patriarchal self' while she realizes that 'the homecoming is very different from what she had imagined'; but her action, in freeing herself from 'the limited space' of her in-laws and from a thoughtless husband who 'uses' her at night, is irrevocable and committed with responsibility and deliberation. In *Daughters of the House* the male protagonist is a symbol of lust and inconstancy, an intruder who violates and impregnates the young girl Madhuchanda, who, as the resolute female protagonist shuns his hand in marriage while giving birth to a female child as an unwed mother. This repudiation of the need for a husband or a father heralds the genesis of a new era of post-modernism in women's literature.

Sunita Jain's poetry has a novel streak of mellowed grievances which easily blends with her hopes and fantasies of a better world. There are two parallel voices that are discernible in her work.[9] Through the first she makes a slightly perturbed but generally calm statement of the insecurities and injustices in a brutal world. She utters a plaintive but strong note in the poem 'Father':

> Unloved I grew as earth sometimes grows to be a tree.

In this line and in such other contexts there is a latent implication of a woman's strength and tolerance like that of the earth or a tree. Through the second she manifests a poetic predilection for the inner world of peaceful retreat from the outer sphere of cruelty:

> soon the sea will roll back
> the shell close upon itself
> the vermillions burn
> till the colours of flame
> are ash.

Instead of resorting to virulence or rebellion she reveals her faith in the quiet, inner world of the woman, beaming with sunlight, resilience and dreams. In the poem "What is it" she looks at her daughter and keeps 'wondering on which peg/she hangs her dreams.' Dreams and tender fancies are symbols, not of fragility, but of resuscitation and of life in a woman's world, often invaded by apathy and harshness

> I dreamed my innocent dreams,

smaller than sparrows,
but like a rocket, life took off.
It's not a hut, but a spacious house
where the food is placed on the table
and no one waits for any one...

In such postcolonial poetry the microcosm of the woman's private world is successfully connected with the jet-age macrocosm lying outside. The 'rocket,' apart from implying speed and rapid progress, also has buried connotations of uncertainty of destination, death and destruction. Yet the 'sparrow' becomes a more meaningful and dominant image in projecting the natural warmth, strength and beauty of the woman's world.

A strong note of feministic outcry is detectable in Malika Amar Shaikh's poem "Megalopolis" (*In Their Own Voice*, ed. Arlene Zide, 1993) which is a candid and bare statement of the physicality of a woman used, more often than not, as a refuge or a therapy by unhappy, incomplete men:

One whole woman
Complete with a uterus . . .
You come to her bosom and thighs to look for the meaning of the world
Or the answers to your questions
Or just to kill time
Or for variety . . .
Wife, mistress, whore
What's the difference.

Lakshmi Kannan's poem "Draupadi" uses the epical story of Draupadi's public stripping and dishonour by the law-makers of a patriarchal society as a metaphor for the injustices still meted out to the female race, though in subtler ways. The 'pain' according to Kannan 'was more tangible years ago' reflected in 'the swollen blue and purple bruises' on the female body; but the woman-question still remains unresolved, despite the various activities and organizations who act only on paper:

Once more
stripped to the raw nerves
Draupadi is bared in books,
papers, case studies . . .
her heart arrested at a still point in history.

Imtiaz Dharker in her poem "Purdah" speaks of the cruel constraints in the life of a woman 'as if she were a clod of earth/. . . passing constantly out of her own hands.' Rajlukshmee Debee Bhattacharya uses a kind of feminist intertextuality in her poem "Cophetua" to explore and evince a similar feeling of restriction to feminine freedom; in this poem the beggar maid is undermined and subjugated, with limitations set on her life and love through the male-dominated institution of King Cophetua's royalty:

> Your voice cracked the shell of the sky
> Your guards . . . their arms stiff
> Under silks and pearls. . . .
> The palace gathers itself around me. . . .
> Emperor, your velvets rope my flesh.
> Somewhere a bed of rags, empty
> Mourns for you and me.

In the final analysis there is an increasing immediacy and openness noticeable in women's writings today; there is a certain confessional and empirical element which was absent in the earlier phase. In this new feminine literature the personal short lyric and the short story genres show that it is more "associational in organization than logically structured"[10]; the attitudes are more frank than ever, the themes such as those of sexuality, conflicts, promiscuity, interrelationships, guilts, shames, rebellions, love affairs are surprising and revelatory and the poetic/literary structures are more experimental than ever. There has been a steady progression from abstract nationalist constructions and those related to the woman and her home in the colonial days to a much wider canvas of the totally liberated and humanized female being in perceptive interaction with the greater world around her. The woman writer's imagination is engaged in a more detailed and focussed reality—the diction is more direct, colloquial and contemporary, contributing to the vitality and sharpness of the texture of the compositions. Hence the distance between the writer's self and her milieu has been eliminated while making her an intrinsic part of the extrinsic as well. In terms of the social and individual consciousness that permeates most of women's literature today, these writers are undeniably the most effective agents of social, political and economic development of the nation during this postcolonial age. It would not be an exaggeration to state that they are the torch-bearers to the twenty-first century. It would be meaningful to recollect, in this context, Anees Jung's poignant lines of tribute to women all over India:

Centuries ago, a king, while travelling through his domain came across people living in dark caves. He was horrified at the gloom and ordered every family to be given lamps and oil to fuel them. Fifty years later he visited the area again and found the caves in darkness. The lamps had been forgotten or were broken. The oil had run out. The king ordered more oil, new lamps. But when he returned to the area the following year the caves were dark once more. The King summoned his minister, a wise old man and asked for an explanation, 'Ah' said the minister, 'you gave the lamps to the men. You should have given them to the women.' The king followed his minister's advice and the lamps have kept burning ever since![11]

NOTES

1. Anita Desai, "The Farewell Party," *The Inner Coutyard* ed. Lakshmi Holmstrom (Rupa, 1994).
2. Malathi Rao, "Jahanara's Tomb," *Woman, Image, Text* (Trianka, 1986).
3. Mikhail Bakhtin, *The Dialogic Imagination* (University of Texas Press, 1981).
4. Lola Chatterjee, *Woman, Image, Text* (Trianka, 1986).
5. M. Prasad, ed., *Contemporary Indian English Stories* (Sterling, 1983).
6. B.R. Nanda, ed., *Indian Women* (Vikas, 1976).
7. Lakshmi Holmstrom, *The Inner Courtyard* (Rupa, 1994).
8. Indrani Aikath-Gyaltsen, *Daughters of the House* (Penguin India, 1992).
9. Manju Jaidka, "The Whimper and the Dream," *Recent Indian English Poets* (Bahri, 1992).
10. Bruce King, *Modern Indian Poetry in English* (Oxford University Press, 1992).
11. Anees Jung, *Unveiling India: A Women's Journey* (Penguin, 1987).

Colonization and Literary Relationship: Lalbehari Dey's *Govinda Samanta* and Fakirmohan Senapati's *Chhamana Athaguntha*

ESHA DEY

Colonization is a kind of encounter, no matter how oppressive and demeaning, between what is known as the third world and the first. Quite often it tries to shape a multilingual heterogeneous ethos into a monolingual, monolithic system giving rise to contradictory and conflicting patterns of interaction. Such an encounter may act as an agent of liberation and at the same time because of its very colonial nature subverts the process of development. Lalbehari Dey's English novel *Govinda Samanta* or *The History of a Bengal Raiyat* (1874) and Fakirmohan Senapati's Oriya fiction *Chhamana Athaguntha* (1902), each a pioneering work in the respective field, reveal the paradox of the colonial situation in literature.

Lalbehari's work, as is well-known, won a £ 50 prize as the best novel in English or Bengali for illustrating 'the social and domestic life of the Rural Population and Working Classes of Bengal' offered by a Bengali Zamindar, Baboo Jay Kissen Mookerjee of Uttarpara in 1871. The novel presents, in sixty chapters, a sort of epic narration of the history of an average Bengali peasant, Govinda Samanta from birth to death minutely described with a huge mass of concrete, almost ethnographic, details about his social, economic and cultural environment and life-style. The focus falls on the hero who, enjoying all the bounties of a rich agrarian existence with its traditional code of rights and duties, participates in a humble way in the new sensibility which is the result of his father's definite break with the Hindu orthodoxy forbidding education for his caste. His brief stint of instruction in Bengali and native arithmetic is enough to provoke a sense of injustice at the violent economic repression of the upstart Zamindar who is actually a middleman empowered by the new revenue system of the British colonial administration. The course of collision leads to his economic ruin which accelerates with demands of religious/social observances and natural calamities. Sinking deeper and deeper in debt he is finally reduced to the great indignity of a landless labourer. Uprooted and destitute he dies in an alien place away from all that he inherited.

The narrative not only presents the most comprehensive document of the contemporary peasant life in Bengal, but also bequeaths in the form of the hero an archetype of the Indian peasant—an honest, diligent, deeply religious tradition-bound family man crushed by a ruthless authority and an equally cruel nature. In innumerable succeeding works in various Indian languages closely followed by the mass media, this archetype today is so dominant and familiar that it is used even by foreign writers in their delineation of the Indian poor ((e.g. Dominique Lapierre's Hazari Pal in *The City of Joy*, 1985). A close analysis of the text however reveals a contradiction in the core of social consciousness which articulates protests against a system imposed by a colonial power and at the same time clings to those very traditional mores which are largely responsible for such repression. Govinda, his brother, the black giant Kalamanik and their young friends are vociferous in denunciation of the exploitation and injustice unleashed by the landlord, so are his brother-in-law and his villagers against the alien indigo-planter. In both cases, the resistance fails miserably because of the defects inherent in their very mode of existence as illustrated in the rudimentary technology of armed defence, restricted social consciousness in the absence of unity and ambiguous ethics which justifies lies. Much that we admire the courage and nationalism of the author who in the heyday of British imperialism dared to record his protest and indignation so loudly and clearly (e.g. 'those horrible engines of oppression were allowed by a Government calling itself Christian, to grind to the dust many millions of probably the most peaceful people upon earth'), it has to be admitted that the consciousness of such an alert and erudite mind was severely restricted by the very colonial nature of the expression. Despite all the turbulence of social and religious reform that was going on all around him in Bengal, and of which he himself was an active participant, he was forced to strike a defensive stance in those very aspects of Hindu life because he wrote in English and addressed himself to the colonizers as readers. The awareness of Bengali society directed towards the problem of poverty, the tyranny of authority and restriction of individual freedom, which had started to find expression in the medieval Bengali narrative form of *Mangal-Kavya* now turned to an in-depth self-analysis in the nineteenth century focusing as much the traditional core of oppression as the repressive foreign domination. Dramas like *Neeldarpan* 1860, *Buro Shaliker Ghare ro* 1860, *Biye Pagla Buro* 1866, *Jamai Barike*

1872 exemplify this dual concern. The social question in fact gradually assumes dominance so as to shape and influence even not-so-realistic forms of expression. Therefore if a Bengali writer in English identifies himself only with some aspects of the contemporary situation and defends the traditional machinery of oppression, the objectivity of his analysis as also the sufficiency of his awareness is seriously affected, e.g. Lalbehari's strong and repeated defence of the status of the Hindu widows (except the extreme case of burning on husband's pyre), portrayal of the efficacy of exorcism and the justification of caste system. One of the main targets of the contemporary reform movement was the Hindu orthodox compulsion which enjoins performance of innumerable rituals daily as well as at every conceivable Govinda's performance of all such rituals with full approval indicate the regressive counterpoint of this discourse. When Govinda under severe economic restraints, performs mother's funeral ceremony "with suitable pomp," the author is clearly forced into a conscious defence. "English reader may exclaim, 'Govinda must have been a fool to spend money on such an occasion, especially as he had no money.' Whether he had money or not is beside the point. Spend he must, whether he had it or not. The customs of the country, the laws of the Hindu society, of the Hindu religion, all demand it." So the portrayal of such "demand," is whitewashed, idealized even to the extent of glorification. When Govinda performs the required rite at the rebuilding of his cottage, set to fire by the landlord, Lalbehari, himself a Christian and a priest expatiates. "People may call this fetishism if they choose, but it is impossible not to have respect for that deep religiousness which underlies the Hindu character, even in a common Hindu peasant. Though the rites are superstitious, they are not meaningless, they indicate the existence of an essentially noble and supersensual sentiment, they show that, even in an uneducated peasant there is something which could not have been either inherited or developed from a monkey; they are an acknowledgement that human happiness is dependent on the smiles of an unseen power, and that all prosperity flows from the bountiful Author of all good."

Thus the practice and dominance of the colonizer's religion and language supposedly modern tend to reinforce the archaic and orthodox mode of the colonized existence inspiring a new defence of the enemy within. A Caliban using his master's tongue can rarely attain the master's freedom. However it is significant that if such a writer sufficiently assimilates the master's literary convention so as to utilize it for his specific purpose, he succeeds in starting a new tradition. Lalbehari's extensive use of Bengali words and phrases in his English text (requiring a lengthy glossary) imparts not merely local colour but builds up step by step painstakingly a fictional world with a whole set of pronounced differences in thought, emotion and life-style. Although the discourse constantly refers to pre-novel narrative conventions, this linguistic realism is adopted from the contemporary British tradition. It is this element that has been followed by later Indian writers in English and now forms a canon of 'Indianness' and even 'ethnicity.'

The interaction of socio-economic context and multilingual situation finds no less an interesting expression in Fakirmohan Senapati's *Chhamana Athaguntha.* The Oriya novel seems to have been inspired by the English text of the Bengali writer for it also purports to show the oppression of a common villager by the existing system. Here too a measure of land (*Chhamana Athaguntha*, i.e. 6 acres and 8 decimals) the inheritance of Bhagia, a weaver, is appropriated by Mangaraj a landlord-cum-moneylender through chicanery and strong-arm tactics. In both, victims are totally ruined. Settings are also similar like the big tank with a legend, deity in a consecrated tree, gathering of women at watersteps full of gossip, the same type of ghosts haunting the environs and so on. Minor characters too suggest actual contact—in both a widow becomes *vaishnavi* to live with a guru, the *vaidya* or traditional doctor is found thoroughly useless in crisis. Indeed the debt goes deep into the very concept of the works as both are conceived as serious imitations of social reality in a form which displays the authors' intimate knowledge of the common rural life of the time. Fakrimohan's dependence on the earlier work does not rest on mere speculation, for in his autobiography (*Atmajiban Charita* 1917) Lalbehari's *Govinda Samanta* happens to find actual mention among the few English books he set himself to study.

Analyzed as an artefact we find that most elements found originally in *Govinda Samanta* have undergone remarkable transformations. Events and characters combine to produce new meaning. In *Govinda Samanta* Kalamanik is beaten to death by landlord's goons. In *Chhamana* Gobra Jena imprisoned for perjury is beaten to death by the fellow prisoners who had their own accounts to settle with him. In *Govinda Samanta* a small girl robbed of her ornaments is killed and thrown into water. In *Chhamana*, the leading female Champa is murdered by her accomplice, her ornaments filched by the investigating police (along with the sweepers cutting off her feet to get the heavy anklets) and her decomposed mutilated body thrown into river. The people and the police unitedly get rid of the corpse describing her interestingly as "a beggar woman from the West" i.e. a Hindi-speaking outsider. She is supposed to have died of snake bite. In the earlier work

Govinda's brother Gayaram too died of snake bite. In both, police officers are Muslims, corrupt, wily and contemptuous of the local Hindu population. But in *Chhamana* the report of the officer is a classic in its half-caste style, loading Oriya with Urdu words. This hybridization obviously indicates a linguistic and historical context in which the moribund state of the Oriya society as well as culture made such distortion possible. Perhaps the differences in actual life as well as in the attitudes of the authors led to the transformation of the elements.

This difference is most visible in the description of the village life. Take for example, the market and the school. In both, the market is a field of Zamindar's exploitation. But in the Bengali village the agrarian produce is so overwhelmingly rich that none minds. Besides, such gathering also offers an opportunity to the German missionary to preach in Bengali and distribute Bengali pamphlets though no one is convinced of the greatness of "Jesu Kristo," everyone scrambles to receive a free copy of the pamphlet *Satyasraya* (Shelter in Truth), as does our hero. This readiness to respond to any exposure from the unknown even to an alien religion is completely absent in the Oriya village. The kind of instruction available in the two is another pointer. There are two *Pathshalas* (native schools) in the Bengali village—both economically self-supporting and vigorous—one for the upper castes, the second open to all. The first one emphasizing Sanskrit, is criticized for its weakness in Bengali, the second one, reportedly, provides better elementary education than even the English schools of the city for it not only teaches Bengali and native arithmetic but also official correspondence in the mother tongue and thus prepares the pupils to face life. In the Oriya village the traditional *chowpadi* is in a decadent stage and continues to teach the Brahmin boys the same old Sanskrit texts without any relevance to the contemporary reality. These brahmins are so debased in their characters so insignificant in their learning that they exert no influence, exercise no power over the people. A Hindu social order where brahmins no longer function as leaders, presents a structure in which the centre has ceased to hold. This fundamental absence of cohesion in a tradition-bound rural existence suggests a hard core of profound moral degeneration which does not seem to affect the Bengali village. Indeed Fakirmohan's community existing on the periphery of the British empire revolves round the decadent precolonial Hindu matrix. So his old, legitimate, landowners Baghsimghas, who are contrasted with the neo-rich Mangaraj, still enjoy the unpaid labour of the people, whose ancestors have been their subjects, without any qualm and their household welcomes Mangaraj's emissary, Champa in disguise, only because the proverbial Hindu greed readily accepts a woman bejeweled and well-dressed, bearing a large quantity of eatables as gifts. The difference between the old and new centres of power lies only in degree. The 'good' zamindar in *Govinda Samanta* too is contrasted with the new villain of a middleman. For he gets educated and finally rids his subject of the indigo menace. So the protest of Madhab, Govinda's brother-in-law who was killed by the planter, does not after all, end in futility. But the death of the victims in Fakirmohan holds out no hope of a future social change.

Apart from the wide variance in the degree of socio-ethical evolution, there appears a fundamental difference in the ethos of the village life. The Bengali village obviously enjoys a high quality of life with a bountiful nature (as we find in repeated descriptions of good and plentiful meals), enriched by supportive relationship among individuals who try to cooperate in time of need and participate in healthy communal activities like games, as customary here as the Hindu rituals. In short it is a vibrant and living entity interacting with the outside world. The Oriya village on the other hand is a closed entity existing on the level of subsistence, dominated by a miser and philistine demon of acquisition. People fear him so much that there is hardly any breath of protest; whereas in the Bengali village the miser moneylender is often socially boycotted. The human qualities are virtually absent in the Oriya presentation which shows self-interest as the only motive, deception the only principle of communication, compassion and camaraderie almost unknown. Even marriage and family, the loudly-proclaimed Hindu bastion of orthodoxy, are utterly debased. If the victim-couple are happy with each other they are often subject to satire. Clearly the generic term 'Indian' applied to the rural life of different communities in the subcontinent does not suffice. Naturally the presentation of a different reality needs a technique quite distinct from the first.

This difference is crucial. Lalbehari claims to present a 'plain and unvarnished tale of a plain peasant living in this plain country of Bengal . . . told in a plain manner,' whereas Fakirmohan offers a series of dramatic scenes or sketches unfolding bit by bit a sort of crime story piled with a heap of corpses rounded off with a melodramatic conclusion in a style unique in its rich combination of the colloquial and the formal, wit and humor, discursive as well as descriptive. Indeed Fakirmohan's wise decision to come back to Oriya for his creative work after a few attempts in Bengali reveals his fundamental difference from Lalbehari who is relegated to academic oblivion as a faithful and sincere Bengali recorder of contemporary rural life in English whereas Fakirmohan becomes the father of realism in Oriya.

Born and brought up in the Bengal Presidency, Fakirmohan's sensibilities were formed by Bengali language and literature, as his character was strongly influenced by the Brahmo reformation movement of contemporary Bengal. His art too is informed with a moral commitment to portray sin and retribution in a marked departure from the medieval Oriya tradition. It is not impossible to trace the sources of this art in the nineteenth century Bengali sketches of social life and mores like *Hutom Penchar Naksha* (1862) and the early Bengali novels of social and linguistic realism by Pyarichand Mitra (Tekchand Thakur). Indeed a few incidents, character types, turns of plotting in Fakirmohan's novel appear to be directly lifted from Bengali; for instance, from *Alaler Gharer Dulal* (1858) he seems to copy the description of a spoilt child throwing a piece of flaming charcoal into the beard of the Maulavi in order to get rid of him; from Bankim's *Bish Briksha* (1873), he borrows the role of a vamp for Champa and of course the concept and execution of her disguised entry into the Baghsingha household. To the Bengali ear, even his distinctive down-to-earth tone of satire may echo the witty and incisive social critiques of Bankim like *Muchiram Gudr* and *Lokarahasya*. However these evidences of indebtedness do not lessen a whit Fakirmohan's uniqueness in creating a moral narrative out of the contemporary life in Oriya society at a crucial stage of transition.

The first thing that perhaps escapes attention is the vehement and basic nature of Fakirmohan's intense criticism of a decadent ritualist orthodoxy which, as apparent in the portrayal of the servile and ineffectual brahmins, encourages the growth of persons like Mangaraj who is the true son of the soil—greedy, debauched and extremely religious. The victims Bhagia and Sharia do not escape notices that Bhagia is oppressed not exactly by the Zamindari system of the British but by the Hindu traditional practice of the individual as a banking agency. It is in this role that Mangaraj gets hold of Bhagia's land which is actually a free holding mortgaged to him for the purpose of building a temple of the village deity in the expectation of a miraculous cure of Sharia's barrenness. The superstition, blind faith and absence of scientific knowledge that underlie this situation belong very much to the traditional Hindu mode and not a result of any imposed external system introduced by the colonial rulers. Fakirmohan who was a staunch supporter of the modern English education as well as the British rule, is here engaged in a serious critique of the orthodox Oriya society which he knew like the palm of his hand. As such, the sinner or the oppressor becomes the protagonist of his narration, as also in his other novel *Mamu*. The characters, all flat and one-dimensional, are sharply divided into black and white, 'bad' are the tools of tyranny like Gobra Jena the village chowkidar, the wily barber Jaga and of course Champa, an embodiment of evil. Bhagia and Sharia as well as the ignored and humiliated wife of Mangaraj form the 'good' that is the victims. There is no intermediary or qualifying shades of possibilities. The text however proclaims the Brahmo humanistic teaching: "Hate the sin but not the sinner." How can the blackness of the sinner be lessened or minimized? First, we find the victims too pure, too innocent to survive any reality. It takes 2 to 3 hours for them to count one rupee. Their gullibility almost naturally invites criminal attack. So their crisis and destruction are reported briefly and casually as though normal. The actual process leading to their tragic end is neither built up nor shown. Their fate is important insofar as it has any impact on the protagonist. The elaborate description of Mangaraj's grief at the death of his long-suffering wife—based wholly on the author's own thesis on marriage as a state of blessing—forms the watershed after which it is Mangaraj who is slowly made to appear as a sort of victim. We find the functionaries of law and order who have been so long his buddies and cohorts turn overnight into agents of oppression empowered by the British administration. The indifference and impatience of the white judge, the curtness of the white civil surgeon seem to counter their efficiency in finding the extent of Mangaraj's villainy. If the role of Mangaraj in the death of Sharia cannot be proved—as the post mortem shows starvation to be the cause of death—the responsibility seems to lie entirely with these white men, though the witnesses as well as the agents of the crime are all Oriyas. To readers and critics, Bhagia and Sharia personify the oppression of Oriyas by alien rulers. That the core of oppression lies deeply embedded in the indigenous social order itself is of course one of those unpleasant truths which contemporary nationalism hides under a pose of indignant deprivation. The fact that the police prosecutor, Ishan Chandra Sarker is obviously a Bengali and the defence lawyer greedy Ram Ram Lalla has a pronounced non-Oriya name adds a typical Oriya dimension to this portrayal of a supposed miscarriage of justice. In the end Mangaraj appears almost as oppressed as Sharia, thrashed by other prisoners, bitten by insane Bhagia, his landed property appropriated by his lawyer, the family jewellery stolen by the maidservant who elopes with a *Vaishnav* guru chanting 'Hare-Keshto' in Bengali style. As the sins of the past catch up with everyone, a woman like Champa gets of course the worst [her murder is to be the most gruesome end in Oriya literature]. Mangaraj, duly atoned dies a devout Hindu, his dead soul is beaconed by the ever-devoted ever-forgiving Hindu wife's blessed spirit. Fakirmohan's sharp critical analysis of a decadent order inspired by Bengali enlightenment is subverted by the intrusion of nationalism and ends in the most conventional platitude erected by such a dying order. The same intrusion in fact from the beginning has pervaded the text in bits of satiric references to 'modern' life which have mystified Oriya critics for its anachronism. At the end it shapes the artist's mission. If the Bengali influence on Fakirmohan led him to break away from the Oriya medievalist narrow confines of erotocentricity and verbal acrobatics, it is the reaction to the same Bengali domination in the economic and cultural field that inspired his Oriya nationalism and ultimately defined his limits as an artist. So he started the modern Oriya trend of exploiting Bengali literature as source at the same time became an embodiment of nationalism. As the testament of this duality *Chhamana Athaguntha* remains a work of unique importance in literary relationship.

Girish Karnad's *Hayavadana* and *Nagamandala*: A Study in Postcolonial Dialectics

A. JAGANMOHANA CHARI

There is no gainsaying the fact that the Indian psyche has been reeling under the colonial burden of the past. It is compounded of the effects of the alien rule and the oppressive ethos left over from the *varnashrama dharma*. What appears to be at work in consequence in the present day Indian culture and literatures weaving the webs of hegemonistic structures is an imperialism of the ruling class ideas both of the west and ancient India.

The Indian bourgeoisie-comprador and brahminical in character and interests—became a willing prey or an easy collaborator with the British design to perpetuate their economic hold over the people of India since the middle of the nineteenth century. As a result the new entrepreneurial middle-class which emerged in India, taking its succour from the traditional mores while absorbing the contemporary post-Enlightenment Western ethic, found itself in a division. Girish Karnad explains this division thus: "whereas in public it [the new entrepreneurial class] accepted the Western bourgeois notions of secularism, egalitarianism, and individual merit at home it remained committed to the traditional loyalties of caste, family, and religion." He further says: "Only a society which is honest enough to face the implications of this division squarely could produce meaningful drama out of it."

It looks as though Girish Karnad is talking of his own predicament as an Indian English playwright. A close look at two of his plays—*Hayavadana* and *Nagamandala*—will also tell us the same. It also presses upon the mind of the reader that he has written the plays not as a matter of self-clarification alone, but as therapeutic device also. In the plays he is seized with the theme of incompleteness as he makes it explicit. He seeks to exorcize himself of this demon of incompleteness by dramatizing the predicament; which is also the predicament of the class to which he belongs.

Let us now have a brief look at *Hayavadana* from this viewpoint. The plot of the play, as everyone knows, is as simple as that of a folk-tale although the playwright crams it with everything in the world. Devadatta endowed with all the accomplishments expected of a brahmin youth falls in love, for the seventeenth time, with an extremely agile and quick-witted girl, Padmini, the daughter of a rich *shresti*. Kapila, the son of an ironsmith with a lithe and handsome body, good in the wrestling pit and extremely devoted to his friend Devadatta for his poetry and wisdom, mediates and arranges the marriage of the girl with his friend. Padmini who seems to possess something of the Kali, the female deity, in her is attracted to the virility of Kapila who also worships her beauty instinctively so much so that she would enjoy his company whenever he came to see her husband. Devadatta becomes jealous and tries to postpone the proposed journey on the cart at Ujjain but with no success on account of Padmini's insistence. On the way, Devadatta decides to sacrifice his head to Kali ostensibly in deference to his earlier vow but in fact, unable to bear the pangs of jealousy. On finding the dead body of his friend, Kapila sacrifices his head too, out of his love for his friend as he likes to tell himself but only to avert the possible ignominy. Padmini who goes in search of the friends stumbled on an opportunity of having the best of the two—Davadatta's head and Kapila's body. Kali the primordial deity favours her with the blessings of life of the two friends. Padmini happens to succeed in transposing the heads with the result that there are two men now, one with Devadatta's head and Kapila's body and the other with Kapila's head and Devadatta's body. Since head is superior according to *Shastras* Devadatta scores a point over Kapila. Kapila is the loser in this ludicrous bargain of mixing up of heads. He has lost not only his body to Devadatta but also his peace on account of the *vasanas* lodged in Devadatta's body. His mundane logic that body being the real person Padmini should belong to him is spurned by both Devadatta and Padmini. Finally Devadatta and Padmini go back to the city where Devadatta enjoys the benefits of Kapila's well-trained body for about a year before it loses its verve. Kapila who feels hurt and cheated remains in the forest to train the brahmin's body dancing by his head like a corpse and shape it into form. Padmini, in the end, cheats on her husband and walks with her child in her arms into the embrace of Kapila who once again succeeds in his effort to "live" in the forest. She claims that child to be the child of both Devadatta and Kapila. The play ends with Devadatta coming in on Padmini and Kapila and fighting a duel with the latter in which the heads roll again.

The child who grows as Kapila's child in the forest to be delivered as Devadatta's at the age of five into the city combines in him the thematic strands of the main plot and the sub-plot. When he is given over to a traveller going to the city to be delivered into the hands "of his grandparents, he is found not to be able to laugh like a human child. He laughs only when the horse born of a princess and *gandharva* cursed to live like a horse until he loved a human, laughs a real laughter in his attempt to make the child laugh.

This story in which folk conventions and motifs are used in plenty holds out the possibility of several layers of meaning such as: (1) man's quest for his origins, (2) status of friendship and love, (3) city versus forest, (4) innocence versus guilt, (5) the primordial relation between man and woman, (6) life versus death, (7) man's struggle for completeness, and so on. Nevertheless, what Girish Karnad has consciously tried to create, it appears, is the last of the above-mentioned themes. But if one deconstructs all these, one could arrive at a space which throbs with a neo-colonial dialectic which is brought into being by the absorption of metaphysical traditions of both the West and ancient India. What is common for these traditions is the world view which splits everything into the real and the ideal and looks upon the latter as more valid. It also views things or phenomena as given and disconnected. It has come to be called metaphysical dualism which justifies the existence of classes or castes. In its discourse, it is status-quo-ist. But when confronted squarely it also gives the lie to itself.

In Karnad's *Hayavadana*, the metaphysical dialectic or discourse we come across consists in its essence in the statement made by Devadatta: "According to the *Shastras*, the head is the sign of a man" and also in the text uttered by Padmini: "Must the head always win." If we examine the logic which is pre-given, Devadatta's head should succeed in explicating Kapila's body to his and Padmini's satisfaction, after it is hooked on to Devadatta's head. But after about a year his head fails to enjoy the liveliness of the body. Its litheness begins to wear off owing to the lack of physical labour. Consequently, Devadatta loses Padmini to Kapila once again. And Kapila who finds the brahmin's body a drag and a torture trains it by hard physical labour in the forest. And he "lives" unlike his friend. The subversionist folk element in the play also plays on this text "live" into a disruptionist comment on the quality of life of the city, the knowledge of *Shastras* and *Varnashrama dharma* as dead and oppressive. The question is: how has he come to live? Not by head as Padmini seems to think but by labour. The idea of metaphysical dualism of body and head corresponding to that of real and ideal is not merely unscientific. Conferring superiority on head entails negation of body which starts off a self-negating conflict between the two. The relation becomes one of opposition and oppression instead of dialectical unity. If we translate it into social terms, a brahmin head is the repository of abstract ideas divested of all sensuousness. Abstract ideas of ritualistic nature which tradition has sanctified are useful for a brahmin like Devadatta in exercizing authority or dominance over a non-brahmin like Kapila and also a woman like Padmini. But he finds in reality or in his experience sensuous pleasures of the body inescapable. So he discovers the lie inherent in his own being. He refuses to come out of it because it represents the mystique on which his class/caste thrives. Kapila too, who has bowed to the hegemonistic mystique yields to the lie and sacrifices his own passion for Padmini, when he cuts off his head in Kali temple.

That both of them—Devadatta and Kapila—are victims of the metaphysical mystique which is at the base of *varnasharma dharma* is aptly conveyed by Kali to Padmini in the dilapidated temple. Kali does not hide her disgust in saying that both Devadatta and Kapila "were lying to their last breaths." Only Padmini is found to be sincere in her selfishness and she speaks the truth when she mixes up the heads.

Woman, like Padmini, is yet another victim of postcolonial dialectic. If Kapila the ironsmith is oppressed by the hegemonistic violence of the ruling class ideology, Padmini, the woman is also repressed by the power of patriarchal values of the ruling class ideology. But she appears to be relatively more free and more capable of distancing herself from the hegemonistic contexts. She may rest content in her consent to the hegemonic structures; yet she adopts the more indirect mode of facing up to reality. Owing to her naturalness and to the degree in which she is away from the matrix of power, only she can be sincere to herself.

Similarly, Padmini in *Hayavadana* acts within the space the post-colonial dialectic allows her. Originally she tries to save the situation for herself by mixing up heads. But as she herself subscribes to the ideology of head, not physical labour, which is against nature, she becomes a victim of the lie herself. When she realizes her mistake, she practises deceit on her husband whom she sends to fetch dolls for her child from Ujjain and she herself makes yet another symbolic journey to Ujjain, i.e. to Kapila and his abode in the forest.

This in the language of dialectics of nature also amounts to the rejection of the metaphysical dialectic or the brahminical ideology. That being determines consciousness, not the other way round is vindicated. But the author Girish Karnad does not rest the problematic in the play at that. He stretches it on account of his collaborationist hegemonistic psychology beyond the natural bounds of the story and sacrifices the men at the altar of status-quo-ist values and drives the woman to *suttee*. But the subversionist folk-tale nature of the story gives the lie to the author's ideology, all the same.

Same thing happens in *Nagamandala* too. The postcolonial matrix embedded in the play opens up yet another space for the working out of the theme of patriarchal oppression.

The concept of ritualistic purity of the metaphysical tradition has structured the hierarchical vertical line-up of gods at the top, men below and women still underneath. So with the classes and castes. The plot of *Nagamandala* unfolds thus: Appanna marries and fetches home Rani to keep her locked inside the house. She is allowed only to cook his lunch. He exercises absolute supremacy over her while he arrogates to himself the power of spending the night with another woman. This vulgar display of power instead of love and treating woman as a disposable object accrues to him owing to the postcolonialist ethos and the mystique of tradition.

Kurudavva who plays the Kali in this play provides Rani with some roots with pseudo-magical powers to make her husband come round to her. But in her fear of, as well as for, her husband, for the magical potion she has prepared out of the roots is poisonous red, Rani pours it into the anthill in which lives a king-cobra. The aphrodisiac works on the Naga and he tuns into her lover. Naga begins to call on Rani in the shape of her husband in the nights and makes love to her. Appanna who notices Kurudavva and her son near the house keeps a watch dog. Later he keeps a mongoose to keep off the snake. Naga destroys both the watchposts by killing them.

Rani becomes pregnant and she thinks she has conceived for her husband, Appanna. The husband comes in on her secret eventually and accuses her of infidelity. She is put to test in the presence of the village elders. Naga comes to her in the shape of her husband once again to tell her that she should opt for the snake ordeal to escape punishment. That is, she should put her hand into the ant-hill, pull the cobra out, take her oath by the Cobra and "speak the truth." The cobra will not bite her if she speaks the truth, he tells her. Truth is what she believes the fact to be, in her innocence.

When exactly Rani perceives that the man who comes to her in the nights is not her husband Appanna but the cobra in his shape is never the moot point here. The woman in her might have experienced it through and through—as the difference between love and authority of one and the same person, her husband. The dichotomy of lover and husband is in the tradition she has inherited. When she discovers in her experience in the end the difference between Naga's love and that of her husband the feeling of experience hardly crosses the threshold of her consciousness because her experience or her head or her consciousness hardly matters in the world of patriarchal hegemony. In fact, it had already been decreed as a taboo by the dominant set up.

The test of her fidelity, after which her husband, a victim of metaphysical mystique himself will become her slave for good—is a lie which gives the lie to the lie or mystique itself. Thus, the negation is negated for a moment. And the woman takes it out on the husband by making him agree that their son should perform the rituals for the snake that dies like a real lover in the coils of her hair.

As it occurs in one of the folk-tales blended into the play, "'The Story' in the form of a woman dressed in a new colorful sari, 'the song'" tells the story of Rani, Appanna, and Naga to the playwright. He snatches the opportunity of listening to it in a bid to escape the curse of death for the sin of boring his audiences, by keeping himself awake for at least one night as is enjoined on him. Thus the story of *Nagamandala* is the story told by "The Story" of the folk tradition which opens up enough space for the writer's predicament, both as man and playwright to place in the context of postcolonial dialectics.

Struggle for Survival: A Study of Ama Ata Aidoo's "Three Poems for Chinua Achebe"

G. SUDHAKAR

The long cherished freedom has failed to provide decent rulers to the people of African countries in the postcolonial era. The hypocrisy of nationalist leaders like N. Krumah and the rampant corruption and tortures of present rulers particularly in Ghana directed the people to live in miserable conditions. Many a writer delienated this life in their writings.

However Ama Ata Aidoo and Efua Sutherland are the women writers of Ghana to deal with the problems of the influence of neo-colonialism and its aftermath on the people in the present African countries. Aidoo all the time and in all her works dealt with the themes such as prevalence of hypocrisy and corruption in the present society and the impact of imperialism on the people. Aidoo as a committed writer of the black believes that few writers of Africa, such as Achebe and Ngugi wa Thing'o have come up to reverse the created low opinion of Africa in their writings. Aidoo feels that people should protest and fight against the imperialist forces, corruption and hypocrisy to liberate themselves from these alien influences. In one of her interviews Aidoo says: "It comes with freedom—a certain type of freedom which I think no black person in this world has right now. . . . I cannot see myself as a writer, writing about lovers in Accra because you see, there are so many other problems."[1] This essay makes an attempt to critically examine Ama Ata Aidoo's "Three Poems for Chinua Achebe" to assess and evaluate the socio-cultural and economic life of the people of African countries in general and Ghana in particular in the postcolonial era.

"Three Poems for Chinua Achebe" is written in three parts and each has its own title. They are stringed together by means of a running theme. All the poems reveal the present status and miserable plight of the people of not only Ghana but also Africa in general. In the first poem "Questions—for us: Today's African Leadership" Aidoo expresses her strong concern for the existing state of affairs and the problems of leadership. Native rulers who came into power began to exploit the masses. Consequently some of the responsible thinkers and writers begin to express their anger and protest through their writings. In this connection Achebe asserts, "I believe it is impossible to write anything in Africa without some kind of commitment, some kind of message and some kind of protest."[2]

Aidoo adresses this poem to Achebe, and poses questions to the people of Ghana as well as the African countries to awake the consciousness and spirit so that they could liberate themselves from the clutches of the inhuman and corrupt new leadership. At the beginning of the poem Aidoo recalls the unique voice of the early freedom fighters. She says:

> They say
> all beings
> fight to live
> the mole
> the lion and
> the crow.[3]

In the past the colonized believed in the philosophy of 'struggle for existence,' and thought that without struggle there is no existence. It is the law of nature that the living beings have to fight in the universe to exist and to live. Aidoo too believes that the struggle has brought independence and identity to their wretched life:

> They say
> all creatures
> must fight to be
> in the air
> on land
> in water. (71)

However, in the modern African countries, the state of affairs have changed after independence. Natives who came into power have become despotic and immoral by their corrupt practices. Aidoo criticizes the detestable trend of the new leadership for it reminded one of the miserable past life under aliens. She observes:

> We shoot
> like wild mushrooms
> —in the dark—

sneak up like snakes
claw like cats
pounce
and
trample
conquer
kill
consume
Then we go limp
like wild mushrooms
—at high noon. (71-72)

Leaders who have suffered and fought for freedom, become crazy after money, and power once they got it. They are now fighting against each other to kill and plunder.

At this critical juncture Aidoo questions particularly the oppressed and the others in general to think about their nightmarish past to find out a solution to the new threats from the present rulers:

So
Where do we
come in
who
feel bad
just to be firm?
damn al else?
do our own nice or nasty thing. (72)

She expresses her concern to rekindle the earlier spirit to arouse the consciousness to make the oppressed firm to struggle for an uncorrupt society once again.

To achieve the purpose Aidoo reminds the once unforgettable and dreadful past sufferings and sacrifices which people bore for years together for their freedom from the clutches of colonial rule. She recalls:

Surely my brother
500 hundred years is
too long to taste
the kicks
without a murmur? (72)

The new leaders of independent African countries who are influenced by the taste of neo-colonialism and nepotism start to attack even the lower income people and insignificant tribes at many levels. The ultimate consequence of this trend made people poor and forced them to migrate from their native lands. Aidoo bitterly questions all the people of African countries about this inhuman practice:

And for what
do we still come with cup in hand
begging,
pleading and
endlessly shifting? (72)

Thus she not only sternly criticizes the wretched attitude of present rulers but also extends her sympathy to the oppressed, unwanted, and uncared people. She incites the people by questions such as

Who would have us
be human in a world
of cruel beasts
and even more cruel men? (72)

If the people of their own countries who are in power begin to deceive and deport their people, there may not be any other country in the world to receive them. Besides, the rulers of these countries have no right to sell the future of the people. That is why Aidoo now warns the rulers and asks:

In whose name do we ever act?
whose tomorrow do we sell? (73)

In the light of all these facts Aidoo calls upon the people not to be reticent at the time of protest, and at the same time warns them not to allow the politicians to sell the freedom and the future of their children. Thus Aidoo in her first poem poses questions to the present generation regarding the misrule of the new African leaders.

Aidoo's second poem "Modern African Stories" is in the form of a dialogue. In the poem Aidoo explicitly discloses how the people of African countries had been deported by the ruthless rulers to the unknown lands. She also portrays the miserable conditions in peoples' life caused by the corrupt rulers. She says that though it appears queer, it is a fact in the African countries.

At the beginning Aidoo praises the people who shed their blood for freedom and tilled the lands to make their countries prosperous from the beginning of their life. In spite of such sacrifices for their motherlands, people did not become free from the tyrannical rule of deceitful rulers in the postcolonial era. Rulers forced the masses to shift their places. Aidoo reveals it thus:

> I got deported this morning from
> My home, my village, my country and the land which
> my forefathers and foremothers bled for,
> and tilled from the beginning of time. (73)

Sometimes the reasons cited for deportation by the rulers are silly and baseless. Aidoo writes:

> I look like my Cousin from across the border and
> His President and My Prime Minister
> do not see
> eye to eye (73)

In the poem Aidoo says that although the rulers and the government force the people to flee their lands, there are some committed intellectuals in the educational institutions and in the society who extend their support to the struggle. In fact Aidoo remains uncorrupt and unmoved in spite of the privileges offered by the higher education. Though travelled widely abroad on academic tasks, she is closely attached to her motherland. John Negend writes, "Miss Aidoo is concerned more with what we might call a man's weakness and his alienation from his native background."[4] Aidoo doesn't wish to remain alienated, and likes to overcome the general weakness of everyday life. She writes:

> mind you
> My Brother the Professor protests that
> theoretically and linguistically,
> "it simply doesn't make sense!
> No one can ever be deported from
> their native country." (73)

However, in spite of few committed peoples' struggle and their resistance, threats from the rulers and sometimes from the governments become inevitable. So many freedom fighters are deliberately ignored and made vagrants. They are expected to buy the respectability by mortgaging their self and sacrifice. Sons of the soil have to fight against the rulers for their survival. Sometimes the old factories and homes which were built to provide the wherewithal to the people were burnt. Aidoo narrates it painfully thus:

> I had no time to stop and tell him to look
> around: in a land where
> former freedom fighters
> are vagrants, or buy respectability only
> by guarding the property for those they mortgaged
> their youths to fight against
> the factories and the homes they crawled
> at night in the good old days to burn . . . (73-74)

Thus Aidoo narrates how rulers made the life fearful in the present African countries with their heinous acts.

Aidoo's last poem in the trilogy, "New in Africa" reveals the continuation of the sad tale of African countries for the centuries together. Simultaneously at the end of the poem she also recalls the spirit of struggle in the African countries to resist the suppressing ruling forces.

In the past Europeans occupied the lands of Africa and made the life of natives miserable. They turned the people into slaves to meet their needs and demands. Aidoo writes:

> when
> Time closed in on itself and
> Europe closed in on us, and
> the only new things
> we served ourselves and
> our enemies dished to us
> were very old potions (74)

In the past when the colonizer intruded into the African countries to plunder, to rule, the seeds of revolution and protest sprouted in the people of the soil. At that moment Africans fought the colonizer to get independence and freedom to their countries.

However, the much desired independence made the native rulers take the paths of neo-colonialism. The consequences of it are rampant corruption and nepotism. These factors become powerful weapons in the hands of rulers to enjoy and misuse the government properties. Hypocrisy entered their life-style and marred the morals of public life.

The ultimate change is that African countries are once again made to experience untold miseries at the hands of native rulers. Aidoo laments this and writes:

> —nearly always violent—
> just warmed over
> everyone hundred years or so
> As for Africa herself,
> Conquered
> raped
> re-conquered
> re-raped,
> She wriggles still, just like snake
> before Ananse finished him. (74-75)

In this way African countries which got independence by their struggle failed to reap the expected fruits of it. Independence for these countries proved itself as a short relief for them. Struggle, rapes and captures became part and parcel of the people of African countries.

Being a committed writer Aidoo entreats the people to begin the struggle once again against these false rulers to regain their past glory. Michael Ethereton observes, "She too is a politically committed intellectual, and is concerned that Ghanaian society develops in a way that will most benefit the masses."[5] Aidoo here calls upon the people not to keep taciturn but to fight against the corrupt leaders by 'clear eyed or blind'. She incites the people to gain spirit from their cultural life. The stregnth from the songs and dances of the life is essential to attain the new, and moral independance once again. Their struggle should be like a prayer on their lips forever. Aidoo writes:

> So also struggle on
> —clear or blind—
> sometimes with song,
> often with dance,
> and always
> with a prayer on our lips. (75)

Thus Aidoo suggests the people to endure the movement and strength by making it a part and parcel of their life.

In this way Aidoo's three poems narrate the present state of affairs in the African countries, people's miserable life and agonies caused by the corrupt rulers in the present system. Finally the poem also shows an alternative solution to the worst conditions. It suggests the weapons of 'struggle' and 'fight' to root out the false leaderships in the present African countries and to restore the peaceful life.

NOTES

1. *African Writer Talking*, ed. Dennis Dutchden and Cosmo Pieterse (London: Heinemann, 1977), p. 19.
2. Qtd. Kate Turkingtom, *Studies in English Literatures* (London: Edward Arnold, 1977), p. 8.
3. Ama Ata Aidoo, "Three Poems for Chinua Achebe," *Kunapipi*, 12: 2 (1990), pp. 71-75.
4. John Nagenda, "Generations in Conflict," *Protest and Conflict in African Literature*, ed. Cosmo Pieterse and Donald Munro (London: Heinemann, 1969), p. 101.
5. *The Development of African Drama* (London: Hutchinson, 1982), p. 196.

Appropriation of Land: A Pre- and Postcolonial Reality in Ngugi wa Thiong'o's *Weep Not, Child* and Meja Mwangi's *Striving for the Wind*

JAIWANTI DIMRI

Ngugi wa Thiong'o and Meja Mwangi are the two well-known writers from Kenya. Ngugi is indisputably the most distinguished and powerful writer from Kenya. His tireless fight for the rights of the landless and the exploited, his outspoken criticism of the neo-colonial Kenya which led to his prolonged solitary confinement and exile have contributed to his fame. Ngugi is best known for his maiden novel *Weep Not, Child*[1] (1964) which portrays the landless natives' struggle against the white settlers in pre-colonial Kenya. It is interesting to compare Ngugi with Meja Mwangi, a younger writer, another Kikuyu from Kenya who shares with Ngugi the same feeling of urgency and concern for a society threatened with fragmentation. Mwangi's earlier novels are set in Nairobi. With his considerable experience in journalism, radio, television and films, Mwangi has created a new fictional space for modern African urban life in his novels, namely, *Kill Me Quick* (1973), *Going Down River Road* (1976) and *Cockroach Dance* (1979). But in his latest novel *Striving for the Wind*[2] (1990) Mwangi shifts towards rural Kenyan society in a sleepy laid-back farming enclave on the slopes of the Aberdare ranges in central Kenya in post-independence era. The dispossession of the poor man's land forms the major theme in both these novels. In this paper, an attempt is made to critique pre- and postcolonial Kenya with the help of these two texts.

Ngugi's *Weep Not, Child* deals with the adolescence of a young boy Njoroge at the time of the Mau Mau rebellion in Kenya. The main spring of Ngugi's fiction is the colonial experience of the Kenyans and in this crucial struggle between the colonizer and the colonized, land becomes a significant part of the colonial supremacy and power. Deprived of their land, the natives are reduced to the status of landless labourers.

Land is thus the biggest issue leading to the crisis in this novel. Ngotho, the poor farm labourer narrates the story of his dispossession of the ancestral land by the white settlers with the stoicism and wisdom of a religious saint. "What happened, O Murungu, to the land which you gave to us? Where, O creator, went our promised land?" (25) But his sons, who epitomize the younger anti-imperialist generation, do not accept the dispossession of their ancestral land with the same stoicism and fortitude. Ngugi presents the variables adopted by the black people to regain their land and the reasons as well as the circumstances that ultimately lead to their failure in a dispassionate, outwardly simplistic manner. Kathy Kessler problematizes Ngugi's rendering of the past in his fiction. According to Kessler, the interrogative nature of Ngugi's work does not preclude his commitment to Marxism. On the contrary she describes Ngugi's world as a 'complex and problematic historical world.'[3] Kirsten Holst Peterson too observes the central paradox in the "typology of Ngugi's heroes . . . caught between the two opposing forces for the war."[4]

Ngugi focuses on the failure of the Mau Mau rebellion due to the treachery and infighting of the natives. But one can distinctly perceive the novelist's commitment to vindicate the Mau Mau rebellion. Njoroge, the protagonist and Kamau, his elder brother think that the white people "left their country to come and rob us acres of what we have." (43) Boro, the Mau Mau activist interrogates his father: "How can you continue working for a man who has taken your land? How can you go on serving him?" (27) Ngugi is confronted with the enormous task of creating a national or political consciousness without resorting to propaganda. He has to come to terms with two conflicting visions. He has his emotional commitment to his group, his family of landless peasants, but as an artist he never allows the propaganda to annihilate the artist in him. To quote Peterson: "by stressing the difficulties rather than the success of gaining a political revolutionary consciousness, Ngugi has indicated the enormity of the task undertaken. . . . These early agonizing, born out of anger, and cataloguing the slow and painful birth of a political conviction with honesty and integrity, give us an extremely valuable insight into a decisive moment in the history of an emerging nation." (218-19)

Ngugi interwines the conflict between the white landowner Howlands and Ngotho with the conflict between Ngotho and Jacobo, a rich black landowner. Boro, the Mau Mau activist attains a symbolic unity of purpose in the double murder of Howlands, the white settler and Jacobo, the rich black settler. Ngugi adroitly exposes the Manichean world of conflict between the white settlers and the black people but at a deeper level the battle is diversified and directed against their own brothers. The final dispossession of land transpires through Jacobo who comes to represent to Njoroge the image of all that which had robbed him of victory when the door to success had been opened.

Ngugi's correlation of history with myth is problematic. Carol M. Sicherman has referred to historians who object both to Ngugi's carelessness with details and to his promoting myth as history.[5] She incorporates Carlone Neale's argument to support Ngugi's promotion of myth as history. The writers seek to discover not only what has happened but the ways in which things are felt to happen in history. The intermixing of history with myth helps in precipitating reconciliation between the estranged son Boro and his father on the death-bed. Ngotho's parting words have a historic and mythic undertone. "All right, Fight well. Turn your eyes to Murungu and Ruriri." (124) Boro, the dispossessed son of a dispossessed father, would verily remember the parting words of his father and derive the moral strength to wage war in future from Murungu and Ruriri.

Weep Not, Child delineates the hopes and aspirations of the landless Kenyans in pre-independent Kenya, Meja Mwangi's *Striving for the Wind* depicts the postcolonial rural society in a sleepy laid-back farming enclave in Kambi village on the slopes of the Aberdare ranges in contemporary central Kenya. Gone are the days when "the whole land belonged to white settlers." (30) Uhuru (independence) has come and with it the agents of exploitation and suppression have sweeped roles. Mr. Howlands of *Weep Not, Child* is now supplanted by more formidable Baba Pesa who owns three hundred acres of land and aspires to appropriate poor Baba Baru's ten acres of land to complete the Pesa empire. Baba Pesa surpasses the likes of Howlands in his legendary ruthlessness and shrewdness. He treats his fellow villagers with utmost contempt and disdain. "Baba Pesa was in the process of making worms out of everyone, turning them into creatures so tiny you couldn't see most of them couched behind the beer bottles he had bought for them." (64) Mwangi comes to grips with the inequality, the injustice and poverty that are often taken for granted in parts of rural Kenya. The novel presents a poignant portrait of contemporary Kenya where the gap between the land-owners and landless labourers is widening day by day. "Selling bit by bit, they ended up landless in Kambi village struggling as labourers and village beggars." (15) Juda, the commentator/protagonist is highly critical of modern equipments like tractors and chemical fertilizers in a society of poor farmers who are getting poorer day by day in spite of strenuous work while Baba Pesa's estate is fast devouring the shambas.

Juda Pesa, the visionary, semi-mad university graduate is far more fortunate than his counterpart Njoroge in *Weep Not, Child*. His utopian dreams are partially fulfilled and his father has to succumb to his will towards the close of the novel. He wouldn't thus allow his father to prolong his exploitation of the poor villagers and appropriate their money and women—both embodiments of power and authority. For the larger part of the novel, his discourse seems to have been wasted away among the village scoundrels and drunkards. But the subversion of the pattern critiques the contemporary scene. The unavailability of diesel and the impending threat of drought enforce Baba Pesa to work with Baba Baru whose ten acres of land he had always transpired to appropriate. The subversion of another situation leaves him defeated and humiliated. Juda, his son, agrees to marry young Margaret, Baba Baru's school-going daughter who is impregnated by his father and strange relationships might have evolved out of this alliance but the novelist tacitly avoids such a possibility by causing Margaret's death in childbirth. Nevertheless Baba Pesa's heroic efforts to transport the victim to the hospital under heavy odds is invariably commendable. The novel has a suggestive, wishful ending. Baba Pesa has to relent to the familial pressures and circumstantial situations.

Different people have merged from the colonial situation with varying awareness of the opportunities open to them. It is interesting to compare Mwangi with Ngugi. The episodic construction of his novel makes it easier to read it and it is far more easier and simpler than the mythical recreation of Ngugi's vision. Mwangi shows people adrift in an economic disorder and stresses the need of integrating the fast disintegrating rural communities. Both the Kikuyus share the same feeling of urgency and apprehension about a society threatened with fragmentation. Frantz Fanon[6] too had warned against an over-enthusiasm about post-Independence circumstances. Edward Said[7] has pinpointed the limitations which colonial consciousness imposes on a nation. There have been different phases of colonial consciousness in the postcolonial literature. Ngugi's *Weep Not, Child* refers to what may be described as the "oppositional" or "confrontational" phase when the imperialist power posed the main threat to the native in pre-colonial era. Mwangi's *Striving for the Wind* makes a transition to the postcolonial world. The peasant in postcolonial Kenya is still poor, landless and exploited—only the agents of exploitation have swapped roles. Both the writers emphasize the need to make the readers look again at contemporary Kenya and posit the necessity of collective commitment. Ngugi dexterously uses history and myth for this purpose. The real fight is not against an outsider but the enemy from within. Ngugi's portrayal of Mr. Howlands, the white settler is most dispassionate. The white man loves the land as his own and the thought of leaving the country of his choice is far from his mind. Juda Pesa has learned both from the wisdom of ancient sages and the education at the university. As Aschcroft puts it: "The post-colonial world is one in which destructive cultural encounter is changing into an acceptance of difference on equal terms."[8]

Susan Bassnett in her book *Comparative Literature* describes postcolonialism as quite distinct from anti-colonialism." *Striving for the Wind* can be read as a postcolonial text that favours cultural encounter and recognizes the plurality of contacts between colonizing and colonized. Thus Juda Pesa's discourse is never anti-colonial. He simply stresses the need for an introspection and he mixes his sermons with the wisdom of village elders and his western education. Nevertheless he wishes to instill the moral in the wealth-thirsty generation of Baba Pesas to abstain from materialism. He describes the moral that a man was truly free and happy only when he had no desire for the things money could buy. Juda's preference to go to India, the mythical land of renunciation instead of America, the land of the rich, critiques the materialism of postcolonial Kenya. The commentator/protagonist's name Juda itself is problematic. Mwangi has thus problematized the role of modern Judas in contemporary rural Kenyan society.

NOTES

1. Ngugi wa Thiong'o, *Weep Not, Child* (London: Heinemann, 1964).
2. Meja Mwangi, *Striving for the Wind* (Nairobi: Heinemann, 1990).
3. "Rewriting History in Fiction: Elements of Post-Modernism in Ngugi wa Thiong'o's Later Novels," *Ariel*, 25:2, April 1994, p. 76.
4. "Birth Pangs of a National Consciousness: Mau Mau and Ngugi wa Thiong'o," *World Literature Written in English*, 20:2 (1981).
5. "Ngugi wa Thing'o and the Writing of Kenyan History," *Research in African Literature*, 20 (1989), pp. 342-79.
6. *The Wretched of the Earth*, trans. Constance Farrington (Harmondsworth: Penguin, 1982).
7. *Orientalism* (London: Routledge and Kegan Paul, 1978).
8. Qtd. Susan Bassnett, *Comparative Literature: A Critical Introduction* (Oxford: Blackwell, 1993), pp. 75-76.

Culture Hiatus and Colonial Hang Over: A Study of Farhana Sheikh's *The Red Box*

SUBHASH CHANDRA

A central element in the expatriate experience (fictionalised by several well-known writers like V.S. Naipaul, Bharati Mukherjee, Ruth Prawer Jhabvala and others) is the cultural space which the expatriates occupy and zealously guard against the onslaughts of the host culture. The identity question, never conscious concern while living in one's own country, assumes paramount importance. While the inevitable interaction results in some mutation/modification in the value system, attitudes and intellectual perceptions of the immigrants, the expatriate writers seem to be keen to protect the basics of their native cultural heritage. To this end, they often depict protagonists in their works who get caught in the cultural flux, experience contradictory pulls and drives, deviate from what has been ingrained in these by their own culture and many times rule the deviation. I intend to explore this dimension of *The Red Box*. Along with the cultural question, I will also consider the ramifications of the colonial mind-set which the expatriates have to confront, if the host country happens to be an erstwhile colonial power (this phenomenon may be observed even if a country has not been a colonial power, but is a white, European country). Colonialism, in its formal form, does not exist any more anywhere, but the colonial attitudes are entrenched and persist with awesome pugnacity in the minds of the people. The complications arising from this often find expression in the creative works of writers.

The technique adopted by Farhana Sheikh reinforces the thematic concern which is formulating conscious postulates about expatriates' identity in an alien land, in which they are trying to strike roots and yet retain some of their own culture. The research project (concerned with the problems of identity of Asian girls) the central protagonist (a Pakistani), Raisa, is engaged in could be summarised in the opening sentence of Margaret Laurence's *The Diviners:* "The river flowed both ways." Like the heroine of *The Diviners,* Morag Gunn, Raisa too moves on two planes, that is, past and present, in a bid to acquire awareness of the essentials of her "self," on the one hand, and on the other to quantify the adaptive changes that occur in the socio-cultural perceptions and behavioral patterns of the immigrants. Raisa's own situation delineates the distance she has travelled from the parent-cultural plank. The catalytic factors are active. Raisa begins dancing during school days and visits the Roundhouse which is described as a "place where a boy smoked pot, drank alcohol, took off his clothes and danced naked for all to see."[1] She gets attracted towards Alex Brown at the Roundhouse and records: "I wanted him to want me," and begins to look at herself through his eyes: "desirable, beautiful, sensual." (200) Similar cultural transformation is witnessed in Tahira, who has lost her virginity to Arif (a Pakistani) and who is afraid of the blackmail by him, though eventually decides to brave it out and gives him a dressing down.

These represent drastic departures from the cultural moorings. Raisa's interviews constitute a narrative device intended to bring out the contrasting viewpoints of the two almost same-age girls, Tahira and Nasreen, who bring to bear different perspectives on the cultural complexities, caused by their expatriate status. While Tahira's outlook has undergone a change (as also noted above) in respect of socializing with the white boys, Nasreen represents the typical Islamic religious stance which places certain restrictions on human beings in general and women in particular. Nasreen believes that mixing and socialising with other men is responsible for unstable and broken marriages, because then women get attracted to other men and vice-versa, which in turn weakens the marital bonds. For her, religious edicts are right prescription for happiness in marriage. She does form part of the group consisting of boys and girls, but that is more out of the uneasy feeling that she would be left out of the circle, if she cut herself off from the group-activities. As against this Tahira is bold, aggressive and more modern when it comes to socializing. Still the novelist does not depict her as a completely changed person. Tahira's self-imposed restrictions of not drinking, smoking and dancing with boys because "it is not O.K." (21) and her disapproval of the English girls "having kids . . . when they're not even married," bring out the two psychic levels most of the expatriates unavoidably live on, even though they might appear attracted and largely acclimatized by the host culture's norms and mores.

Another contrast in the response of fictional personae in *The Red Box* comes from the male and female members of the immigrants. While Raisa's father is a modernised, westernised liberal, her mother remained a conservative, despising and considering as dangerous the English influence. Raisa's mother's indignation with her husband for allowing

Raisa to imbibe the Western life-style is bitter and intense. This makes Raisa (then young and immature) hate her mother for shackling her life. "I hate her, I hate the bitch! I hope she gets killed," Raisa records. The use of the word "bitch" for her mother should be noted for the typical Western influence and vocabulary Raisa has come to internalize. Trivializing the filial relations is typically characteristic of the Western mode of life, which in turn leads to feverish individualism among the children who do not brook any parental interference in their uninhibited bohemianism. In fact, parents come to be regarded as the sore (and sour) adversaries who hinder the fulfillment of young folks' desires. Tahira's father is dead, but he and Tahira's mother had divorced before his death. Tahira's mother (though divorced which is considered an unusual phenomenon among Pakistani immigrants and which is a typical Western practice) feels anxious for her daughter, lest she should adopt the promiscuous ways of the native English girls. Her mind is constantly troubled by such thoughts: "Had the grey car stopped for Tahira? . . . More and more her life had become an endless chaos of worries." (159)

While the immigrants retain to varying degrees the elements of their parent culture in spite of some of the younger set trying to take on the Western modes, the natives, in their turn are shown to be adamantly hostile to the Asians and treat them as objects of fun and ridicule. The Asian immigrants' sartorial appearance, their manners and their behaviour come in for mockery and satire at the hands of the English boys and girls, who never miss an opportunity to throw a snide remark, intended to hurt the listener. The English youth, for instance, call Tahira and Mumtaz (Tahira's cousin) "dirty Paki slags." (53) Tahira bursts out angrily, "White trash, pig, bastards!" (53) Bharati Mukherjee's *The Tiger's Daughter* records a similar incident in which Tara has to confront violence and ghettos in American life. Sarah in Anita Desai's *Bye-Bye, Blackbird* also has to put up with the boys shouting, "Hurry, Hurry, Mrs. Curry!"[2] Farhana Sheikh's observant eye brings into focus the insurmountables, which she thinks for ever will prevent a harmonious fusion of the two cultures. This is reminiscent of E.M. Forster's celebrated novel, *A Passage to India* (it remains to-date a sympathetic portrayal of India, Forster's occasional satirical comments on India notwithstanding) which underscores the problem of the English and the Indians being friendly. In fact, there is a touch of universality in Sheikh's delineation of the expatriate's experience. As in Bharati Mukherjee's *The Tiger's Daughter* and Anita Desai's *Bye-Bye, Blackbird,* we observe the same invincible hiatus distancing the host and the immigrant cultures. Also like these two writers, the authenticity of the felt experience is reflected in Farhana Sheikh's novel, which brings her work on a par with the experienced and famous writers' books, dealing with the expatriates' problems in the countires of their adoption.

II

Apart from the cultural complications resulting from the interaction between the natives and the immigrants, the writer also highlights the colonial attitude, displayed by the English towards the Asian immigrants. Colonialism, we know, was based on the essential tenet of superiority/inferiority of different races. In its morbid form, it led to Hitlerean concept of pure (and superior) race which caused such diastrous consequences to mankind. After the last vestiges of colonialism have been wiped out from the face of the earth, the colonial consciousness is responsible for a particular mind-set leading to snobbery, superciliousness at the social level, and dispossession and deprivation of the immigrants at the political level.

It is through the South Park School, where Tahira and Nasreen study, that the issue of colonial consciousness is brought into a sharp focus. The central episode that makes the school environment surcharged is the discriminatory, biased attitude towards Jamshid Iqbal (a sixth form Pakistani student) who gets involved in a fracas with a white boy and is callously expelled. His career and life are ruined. The charge is that he possessed a knife which could have been used. But no action is taken against the white student, Terry Ames, who also possessed a knife. The reaction of the white students of the school to the incident has a larger significance: "They've got rid of that flash Paki, for good. Serves the bastards right!" (78) And the comment of the Asians is evocative: "The gorrais kicked Jam out'cos he fought back!" (78) The calculated and wilful discrimination practised against the Asians by the school authorities, by an extended meaning, could as well be the discrimination and cruelties perpetrated by the British in India during their rule. The pattern of response aroused among the students also parallels the agitations and demonstrations (which at times turned violent) that marked the independence struggle in India. Logic and rationality become the first casualty, while dealing with the Asians. The power relations being unequal, the students' agitation expectedly comes to naught. Police arrive on the scene. Some of the students are arrested, others run for safety. The demonstrators finally get scattered and the agitation dissipates. Jamshid remains rusticated. A life is ruined. The immigrants' attempt to assert their equality and strive for justice are aborted, even though they are legally and constitutionally as much citizens of the country as the whites are and they enjoy equal rights with the natives, since they pay equal taxes. The South Park School becomes symbolic of the type of attitude that permeates the society at large vis-a-vis the immigrant Asians (and blacks) and the episode snowballing into an explosive situation, crystallizes the feelings on both sides of the divide.

III

Through the evocative symbol of the Red Box, which though chronicles the insults and humiliation of one individual (Raisa's mother), the novelist makes a powerful statement on the plight of the immigrants. Each immigrant possesses his or her secret Red Box, and has to come to terms with the harrowing experiences deeply affecting and dwarfing human dignity, self-respect and sense of individuality. Raisa's mother's condition acquires much wider importance in terms of the lot of other Asians, both old and young. The binary opposition of white/brown (black) that has been perpetuated for ages and the value-judgment that came to be attached to the colours (white connoting virtue, life, cheerfulnes, superiority and the black standing for death, sin, darkness, despair and inferiority) segregated the world into two halves, in the first place and then became responsible for the maltreatment of the supposedly inferior races (the hair-raising accounts of atrocities on the black slaves in the white world are too well-known). In her book Farhana Sheikh seems to attract attention to and hold to criticism this binary opposition which is responsible for the deprivation, insecurity and physical violence against the immigrants in England.

The novel does not hold out any hope for the degraded condition of the expatriates; in fact there is a sense of foreboding in the outcome of the South Park School episode, which also has a larger suggestion inasmuch as the protest proves ineffectual. Jamshid is rusticated. The Headmaster of the school remains adamant. The ending of the novel, which is part of the technique, is not affirmative, since the novel ends on a journey into the past in the form of reminiscences (except for an exceedingly short last chapter). It is a step away from confronting the present dystopian reality, perhaps actuated by the entrenched awareness that the situation is permanent and irredeemable. Another suggestion that is being made in the ending is that it is a one way entry into the Hell that is England. There is no escape, except for mental forays into the regions of the past. Several characters are unhappy in England, but for diverse reasons they are doomed to remain there.

While the value of the novel lies in its authentic delineation of the troubles and travails of the expatriates in London, it suffers from the absence of growth in the vision of the central protagonist, Raisa. No doubt, she is also shown to belong to the group of discriminated people (she is denied the expected job); but Raisa does not register deepening of perception or does not acquire insight into the larger questions of human existence. The dark note on which the novel ends is depressing. Raisa remains single and deprived of her new job; Nasreen comprehends that she would not be able to do well in spite of her knowledge of the syllabus; Tahira and her family are shown as having to work hard to grapple with life. The novel does not renew the spiritual/moral resources of the fictional personae to be able to cope with the thwarting forces, nor does it show any potentially redeeming features in the sombre landscape.

NOTES

1. Farhana Sheikh, *The Red Box* (Calcutta: Rupa 1991), p. 198.
2. Anita Desai, *Bye-Bye, Blackbird* (Delhi: Hind, 1971), p. 37.

Contributors

Rajita Sai Baba, Hyderabad

Laksmisree Banerjee, Jamshedpur

Nilufer E. Bharucha, University of Bombay

Vinita Bhatnagar, Lucknow

A. Jaganmohana Chari, Kakatiya University, Warangal

Subhash Chandra, S.B.S.C, University of Delhi

Seodial Deena, East Carolina University, U.S.A.

Esha Dey, Calcutta

Jaiwanti Dimri, H.P. University, Shimla

Harrichand Itwaru, University of Toronto, Canada

Amina Kishore, A.M.U., Aligarh

Manjushree S. Kumar, Jodhpur

David Myers, University of Queensland, Rockhampton

A.K. Sinha, Patna University, Patna

G. Sudhakar, Kakatiya University, Warangal

Index